Speed Demon

A plain English guide to swimming sprint freestyle

Fiona Holt

Published by Lulu.com

ISBN: 978-1-4092-6791-1
Revised version

Copyright © 2009 by Fiona Holt.
All rights reserved. No part of this publication may be reproduced or transmitted in any form or by any means, electronic or mechanical, including photocopying, recording, or any information storage and retrieval system, without permission from the publishers.

Contents

INTRODUCTION		5
PART I. TECHNIQUE		**7**
1	WHERE TO START?	8
2	FUNDAMENTAL UPPER BODY TECHNIQUE	10
	STROKE PATH	10
	ARM RECOVERY	13
	FINISH THE STROKE	16
	HAND ENTRY WIDTH	16
	LOCKING THE WRISTS	19
3	SPRINT-SPECIFIC TECHNIQUE	20
	STROKE LENGTH	20
	HIP ROCK	23
	STROKE DEPTH	24
	HAND ENTRY DISTANCE	26
4	SO, WHAT ABOUT THE LEGS?	28
5	STARTS AND TURNS	32
	STARTS	32
	TURNS	34
	The almighty arm pull	34
	Chin on chest	35
	Throw the legs over	36
	Foot-plant position	36
	Heels on the wall?	39
	Head tucked	40
	Surface quickly	40
	Use your hands as rudders	41
	Stroke on the lowest hip side	41
6	BREATHING	43

PART II. TRAINING   48

7   THE COMPLETE TOOL KIT   49
     REST   49
     SPEED   51
     FITNESS AND WEIGHT MAINTENANCE   52
     LACTATE TOLERANCE (AND A RACE STRATEGY)   54
     POWER   57
     CHOICE AND ENJOYMENT   57
     TECHNIQUE AND FLEXIBILITY   58

8   TIME MONITORING   60
     You won't learn anything if you don't   61
     Have I warmed up properly?   62
     Am I ill? Should I train?   62
     It gives a psychological incentive   62

9   TRAINING FOR POWER   64
     What is power?   64
     In the pool or on land?   65
     AREAS TO CONCENTRATE   67
     Driving the arm recovery   68
     The underwater pull   71
     The stomach for tumble turns   73
     The hip drive   74
     The legs for starts and turns   74

10   FLEXIBILITY   76
     The muscles have got to be warmed up …   76
     Hold static stretches for a long time …   78
     Do it regularly   78
     AREAS TO CONCENTRATE   78
     The pecs   79
     The hamstrings   80
     The soleus   80
     The deltoids   82
     The quads   83
     Upper back …   84

CLOSING STATEMENT   86
APPENDICIES   87

Introduction

Have you ever gone back to training after a heavy cold and found that your stroke feels diabolical just because you haven't been in the pool for a week or so? I know I have. It is amazing how quickly we lose what is often called 'a feel for the water'. This implies to me that even if your stroke is pure perfection you still have to do plenty of technique work to keep it that way. But is yours perfect? Or do you have a nagging feeling that you are currently physically capable of swimming much faster? In fact only a few weeks ago in training you were flying along, but you just can't pinpoint what it was that you were doing right. If only you had had a race that day you might have swum a huge pb (personal best). *If only you knew what you needed to change to always swim like that.*

That nagging feeling, that annoying suspicion, that you should be much faster is what the first part of this book is all about. It is the culmination of a decade of thought about how to sprint freestyle. I have heard it said that swimming is the thinking man's sport and I totally agree. Like many of my fellow competitors I became obsessional about technique, increasingly so in later years. I have retired now but I cannot let the current clarity of my understanding condense into a blur somewhere in the distant past; so here it is and I hope it helps.

Some of what I want to say is not necessarily new. I have read a few books on swimming in my time and I have read sentences that I am about to rewrite here. However, often I read it only in the sense that I physically read the words. I did not absorb one iota of it. It passed me by for one simple reason — it did not explain why. If we do not understand why we are asked to do something it is fairly probable that we will not persevere with it. I promise you now that this book will not be filled with diagrams you don't understand, forces you can't visualise and muscle groups you've never heard of. There are now a few books available which explain both the how and why of swimming efficiently. As a consequence some have become very popular and rightly so. I have learnt a lot from them. But sprint swimming is not just about efficiency. The body position of a sprint swimmer is prescribed both by the need for efficiency *and* by the need for power generation. I have therefore split my discussion regarding upper body technique into two Chapters. Chapter 2 addresses fundamental freestyle technique that I think most would agree with, and Chapter 3, which is perhaps slightly more controversial, is specifically aimed at sprint freestyle.

Just one piece of housekeeping before I start. Throughout this book, when I refer to an appendage moving backwards or forwards, I am referring to the sensation felt by the swimmer. We know that in actual fact the hand in freestyle exits the water at a point further forwards from that which it entered, but the sensation is still that the arm moved backwards.

Part I
Technique

1
Where to start?

Which is your main source of propulsion — your arms or your legs? Hopefully this is not too difficult as a starter question but if you're not sure ask yourself this — if I sprint 50 m flat out using just my arms and then do the same using just my legs, which swim will be the fastest? The answer is the one with just your arms. The difference is not insignificant. It is huge. The time you can do 50 m freestyle with just your arms will only be a few seconds short of your full stroke pb, but the time you do with your legs will be miles off it; probably of the order of 15 to 20 seconds slower. So, the next question is — which should you work on, your arms or your legs? One logical answer is that you should concentrate on your legs because they are the weakest. I disagree. Although it is oversimplistic to view your total speed as the sum of your arms-only and legs-only speeds (because for various reasons it isn't), it is true to say that your arms contribute a much larger fraction of your total speed than your legs do. Therefore, in percentage terms, any increase in total speed will be far greater if your arm propulsion rather than your leg propulsion is improved. A 5% improvement in your arms will improve your total speed by far more than a 5% improvement in your legs.

To support this idea let me relay a conversation that I had with a certain teenager several years ago after the heats of the 50 m freestyle at the Southern Counties Championships. Her name was

Becky Cooke (now Becky Cooke — World championship bronze medallist). As my legs buckled underneath me and I collapsed onto the seat in the shower at Crystal Palace, she walked in, chatted briefly and then sauntered off (probably to warm up for yet another race). 'How can you stand up after that?' I said. 'Oh, I can't use my legs, they're useless, they don't do anything for me' she replied. Then she disappeared and I was left to commiserate myself upon yet another identical time and the fact that Becky had just beaten me without even using her legs! You are probably thinking 'hang on Becky Cooke isn't a sprinter'. True, she is very much a distance swimmer, but my point here is that she came into the shower after me. She was in a much later heat than me, i.e. she was a lot faster than me. By her standards she may be a distance swimmer but by the standards of most of the girls at that meet she could easily have been a sprinter. Many of us would have been happy to swap our times for hers. She beat us and she did it without using her legs. Of course she is not an international standard sprint freestyle swimmer and that is because you do need immensely powerful legs to be one. Of course you do, and I will explain why later on, but the message of this story is that the place to start is definitely your arms or, more accurately, your upper body.

2

Fundamental upper body technique

Stroke path

For years I swam with my elbow bent so that my forearm was at about 90 degrees to my upper arm — i.e. with my forearm and hand pointing directly at the bottom of the pool; a bit like the legs of a crocodile (Figure 1X). Why? First of all it was what came naturally to me before technical thoughts had ever entered my head. Then, later on, I reasoned that it was the stance I would adopt to do a press-up therefore it must be pretty strong. I read a book on sprint freestyle that supported it. It advocated lying on your front on a surfboard and paddling. Furthermore, one of my coach's favourite exercises was to ask us to place our hands on the edge of the wall of the pool and raise ourselves up repeatedly; this also required a wide, press-up style stance. It was all wrong. Yet looking back I remember another coach once told me, quite correctly, 'bend your elbow'. 'What does he mean?' I thought, 'I am bending my elbow — it's at 90 degrees'. Because I didn't understand what he meant and he didn't elaborate, I rejected it. He meant bend it more (Figure 1). How many times have we read in textbooks that the hand path in freestyle should follow the centre line of the body (with the angle between the forearm and the upper arm at much less than 90 degrees) but then ignored it because we haven't appreciated why? To understand you must start by answering the question — is the freestyle arm stroke a push or a pull?

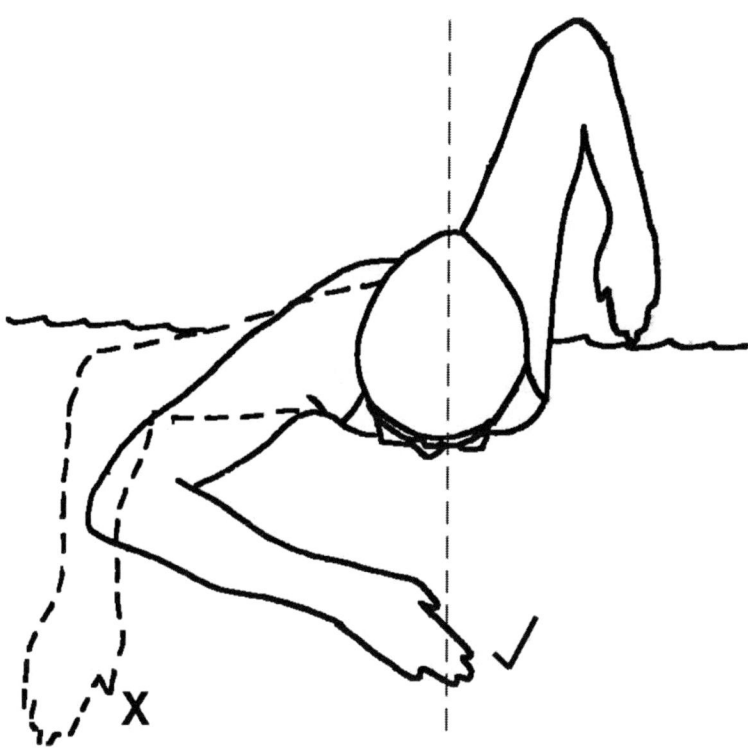

Figure 1. The correct hand path is down the centre of the body with the hand directly beneath the chest. Why? Because the arm stroke is predominantly a pull and not a push.

You may be forgiven for thinking it is a push. After all you *push* against the water don't you? Well, it is true that you do in the latter stages of the stroke, after the hands have passed the lower chest. The majority of the stroke however, before the hands reach the lower chest, is definitely a pull. I make the distinction because pulling and pushing actions employ entirely different sets of muscles. The best analogy I can think of to demonstrate this is to compare a push-up (or press-up) with hauling in a rope that has a heavy weight on the end, such as in the game Tug-of-war. To do a push-up you aim to push your upper body away from the floor and you automatically place your hands shoulder width apart or more. Imagine trying to do a push-up with your hands placed next to each other in front of your chest. It would be considerably harder. But when you haul in a rope you always draw the rope down the centre line of your body, directly towards your stomach. You would never haul in a heavy anchor or pull a heavy church bell by standing to one side of the rope and drawing it out wide to one side of your body. You would be far weaker if you did so. The majority of the swimming stroke is exactly the same as hauling in a rope, but instead of your body being vertical and perpendicular to the rope it is horizontal and parallel to it.

So, from the point at which your hand has caught hold of the water to the point at which it reaches your chest, you should draw it down the centre line of your body as though you are pulling an imaginary rope towards the centre of your stomach. (Another good analogy that I have heard is to imagine that there is a single line of poles sticking up from the swimming pool floor and that you have to haul yourself along through the water by reaching out and pulling on each of them).

After your hand has passed your chest you need to move it out wide for two reasons. Firstly you are now pushing and the strongest stance for that is to keep your hands just outside the width of your shoulders. Secondly, and pretty obviously, you have got to remove your hand from the water without disturbing the movement of your hips.

There is a simple weights exercise that you can do to prove this push versus pull point to yourself. See page 71.

To summarize: The majority of the freestyle arm movement is a pulling action and not a push. The strongest stance for a pull is to move your hands down the centre line of your body towards your stomach. Move your hands out to the width of your shoulders towards the end of your stroke.

Arm recovery

Why do swimmers obsess about stretching their pecs? (the pectoral muscles, or 'pecs', are the ones linking the front of your shoulder to your chest). Go to any swimming gala and you are guaranteed to find competitors strewn all over the place stretching their arms along walls or raising their hands together behind their backs. To reply that swimmers need to have flexible arms is true but it is not really an answer. It just leads to the question — why do swimmers need to have flexible arms? The answer is key to understanding how not to recover your arms. (By recovery I mean raising your arm and hand out of the water and then moving them forwards through the air to prepare to take another stroke).

Once the arm has finished its pulling action the hand has, fairly obviously, got to be completely removed from the water. If you can fully achieve this by driving your elbow and shoulder backwards (which requires the pecs to be stretched) then you avoid the road to disaster; that is to resort to raising the centre of your chest so that your hand can be raised out of the water. Why is this such a crime? Because it violates the golden rule of all sports. If the chest starts rising and falling the head will do the same, and the golden rule is that the head *must* be kept still (except of course to breathe — see page 43). If your head starts moving around then your brain *will* fail to get all the other parts of the body in the correct relative positions (Figure 2).

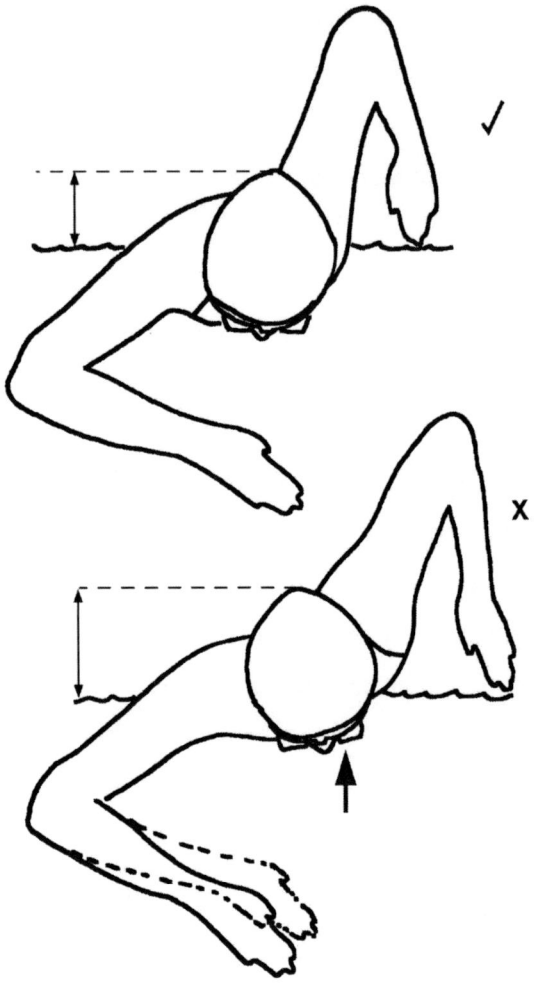

Figure 2. In Figure 2X the swimmer's chest has been raised to help the left hand clear the water. Consequently the head has raised and twisted and the right hand has drifted in the opposite direction to balance its movement. Thus, due to inflexibility in the left pec, the right hand has not pulled along the correct path down the centre line of the body.

Now I am going to guess that you can already get your elbow and shoulder back high enough to recover your hand fully out of the

Fundamental upper body technique

water, or if you can't quite, you roll onto your side rather than raising your chest (Figure 4). I say this because flexibility in the pecs is so fundamental to swimming freestyle that I suspect that people who don't naturally have it simply don't take up swimming seriously. They discover fairly early on in life that it's not the sport for them, though they don't have a clue why. To observe what-not-to-do just go down to a public swimming session and watch. You will see that the majority of the men haul their chests out of the water in a perpetual losing battle.

Men tend to have more tension in their pecs than women. Perhaps its due to their naturally greater muscle mass or perhaps its because the kind of guy that goes to the pool and swims lengths also does a lot of bench press (there is nothing like bench press to tighten up your pecs). Whatever the reason, the average man on the street cannot reach his arm out straight behind him and rotate it in circles properly whereas the average woman, and most swimmers, can. Many sports coaches like to set their athletes bench press. It is of some use to swimmers as it strengthens up the primary muscles involved in the push phase in the latter part of the arm stroke. However, the advantages of any strength gained will be completely and utterly negated if the swimmer does not stretch their pecs properly after each weights session to maintain the flexibility necessary for a correct arm recovery.

The message here then is that practically all of the hand recovery should be achieved by driving the elbow and shoulder backwards. If you are nowhere near achieving this then you should stretch on land until you can (Figure 14 page 79). This is also an appropriate place to add, what I hope will be, the final nail in the coffin for a drill that is a particular pet hate of mine. The one that involves tapping yourself under the armpit as you move your hand through the recovery. Nobody knows why we do it. We just seem to do it because the last coach set it. It's like doing something just because your parents did. It doesn't make it right! If the crucial factor in recovering your arm is to remove the possibility of raising the chest, why on earth would you do a drill that makes you take your hand further out of the water than you need to? It is asking for trouble in my opinion. It saddens me to watch a group of swimmers start this drill in a training session. Their chests immediately start pumping up and down and the amount of white splash in the pool seems to immediately double. Never take your hand any further out of the water than you have to. As soon as it is clear get on with the business of getting it forwards.

To summarize: At the end of your arm stroke most of your hand recovery should be achieved by driving your elbow and shoulder backwards and not by raising your chest. If you cannot do this you should stretch your pecs until you can.

Finish the stroke

I may hate the drill that involves touching the armpit, as described above, but one which is quite good to do occasionally is to tap the side of your leg, at the end of the stroke, before taking your hand out of the water. Why? Because it is absolutely criminal to take your hand out of the water when there is still water left to push against. It's short and sweet but that's all that needs to be said.

Hand entry width

Imagine you are looking down at a freestyle swimmer from the ceiling above the pool. Should their hand enter the water directly in front of their head or further wide, e.g. directly in front of their shoulder? In actual fact there are perfectly good arguments for both.

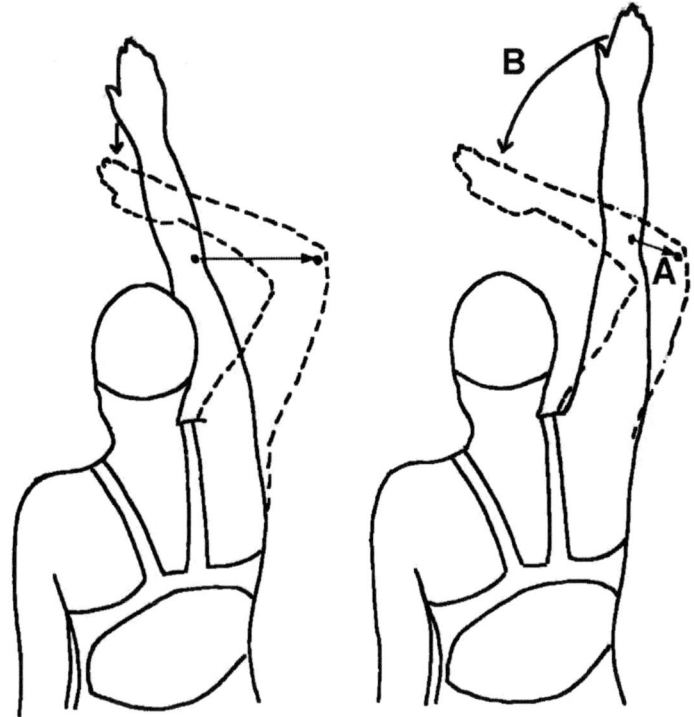

Figure 3. When the hand entry position is wide, the elbow movement (A) is minimised and the water to pull against (B) is increased

The argument for the hand entering directly in front of the head is what I call 'tube swimming'. It is easy to visualise that a cylinder being pushed forwards through the water will encounter less resistance if it has a small diameter. So, moving a chopstick under water requires less energy than moving a tube of Smarties, even if they are both the same weight. So if, when you are swimming, you imagine yourself to be confined inside a narrow tube that you are not allowed to touch the edges of, then your body will encounter less resistance. If you follow this rule then you should make your hand entry right in front of your head. Furthermore, we have established that the hand should travel down the centre line of the body (page 10), so it makes sense to put it there in the first place.

There is also, however, a perfectly good argument for the hand entry point being directly in front of, or even a little wider than, your shoulder. This is to minimise elbow movement.

At the very beginning of a pull the arm is straight. The swimmer now has to make the transition between a straight arm in front of them and an arm bent at the elbow with the hand directly beneath their head. During this phase, whilst the elbow is in the process of bending, the forearm is effectively a small lever where the hand is the paddle and the elbow is the pivot point. (Once the elbow bend is set up, the whole arm becomes a larger, stronger lever with the shoulder acting as the pivot point). A lever is always less effective if its pivot point is moving around. It is much harder to loosen the bolts to change a car tyre if the socket or spanner doesn't fit the bolt exactly. It is much harder to apply the necessary force because it moves around. So, it follows that in freestyle the elbow should be as still as possible during this initial phase. But if the hand enters the water directly in front of the head then the elbow has to slide sideways to allow the hand to pass down the centre line of the body. Whereas, if the hand entry point is wider the elbow can remain relatively (not perfectly) still while the hand sweeps round towards a point directly beneath the head). Plus it has slightly more water to travel through to get there and more opportunity to build up speed. (Figure 3).

To summarize: Experiment with your hand entry position. Are you a tube swimmer or do you need your elbow to be firmly anchored? Perhaps you can find intermediary position that gives you the best of both worlds?

Locking the wrists

I explained above that initially the forearm is a lever with the elbow as its pivot point and that then the whole arm becomes a lever with the shoulder as its pivot point. In actual fact there is a fraction of a second, at the very beginning of the stroke, where the hand is a lever with the wrist as its pivot point. This is the phase we commonly call 'the catch'. (Some people also do it at the very end in which case it is called 'a scull'). During the catch phase the hand has to 'catch' hold of some water for the arm to pull against. At this time, and this time only, the hand will gyrate around the wrist to find water. However, once this brief phase is over, and the hand has reached a point at which it forms a perfectly straight line with the forearm, it should stay in line until the very end of the stroke where it may do the same gyration in a scull. That is, during 99% of the stroke the wrist should become locked as if the joint no longer exists. That way the forearm is at its longest and most effective. Put another way — have you ever seen a rowing boat with floppy paddles? No. So don't let your hand flop around like a piece of cloth in the water. Make a mental note to concentrate on tensing your wrist and locking your hand in a position that makes it a perfect extension of your forearm. You may not realise, until you actually concentrate on it, that you are not quite locking your wrist as strongly as you should be. When you do, it has a tremendous effect on your time. You'd expect any lever to become more effective if you suddenly increased its size by the length of one hand.

To summarize: After you've caught hold of the water, locking your wrists will make the arm pull more effective.

3

Sprint-specific technique

Stroke length

My first, and probably most heretical, opinion is that while the stroke should always be long, a sprinter should not be reaching as far forwards as they physically can. I realise that these days this is a sacrilegious statement so, to quickly appease those who are now throwing my book at the wall, I'll start at the beginning and explain why all freestyle arm strokes should be long.

This needs a return to my rope-hauling scenario. Picture yourself hauling in your rope and this time it's a really long one. You start putting one hand in front of the other at fairly small intervals, but it doesn't take long to realise that you are never going to get the job done quickly with a lot of short pulls. It should be obvious to anyone that to haul in a rope you reach as far forward as possible before you grab the rope. That way you will be able to make much longer pulls. Because each individual pull is longer, within it you build up the movement of the rope to a considerable speed and its momentum may mean it continues moving just a little as you bounce over to start pulling with the next arm. I hope you can visualise this because the situation in the water is identical. All freestyle strokes should be long. If you want to be a successful sprinter you just have to do long strokes more quickly and, if you do them quickly enough, that little bit of momentum I described in the rope is the equivalent of you continuing to drift forwards once your pull is finished.

I would now like you to visualise another scenario. You are in a rowing boat. You reach out forwards holding the end of a single oar and make an almighty long pull on it. It works perfectly and after a few of these long pulls you are soon cruising along on the water. But the boat starts to sink. As it does so, you and your hands gets lower and lower, nearer to the level of the water surface. You find it increasingly difficult to paddle because so much of the oar is immersed in the water. Previously it was just the paddle at the end that dipped into the river, but now that you are low down practically the whole of the oar is lying in the water. It is simply too heavy to lift. You eventually give up.

When you are swimming freestyle your arms are levers just like the oars of a rowing boat. The job that your hands do when you are rowing is the same as the job of your shoulder when you are swimming. They are both the fulcrum or pivot point of the lever. In my rowing scenario, when the boat began to sink, the lever (the oar) required far more effort to work. In the same way, if a swimmer's shoulder sinks it requires more effort to pull the upper arm and the shoulder itself through and out of the water. But if the shoulder is high in the water the arm can work more powerfully.

So you might now be forgiven for thinking that no swimmer should ever submerge their shoulder. There's a catch. To reach a long way forwards and make a stroke as long as possible (which we know is desirable from our rope-hauling scenario) you have to submerge your shoulder. You literally turn on to your side to reach as far as possible and your shoulder sinks. In a nutshell, there is a trade off between the gain you make in terms of the length of your subsequent pull and the loss in power you experience by submerging your shoulder (Figure 4).

It is my opinion that if you are a distance swimmer it may well be worth submerging your shoulder and reaching as far as possible to get the benefit of stroke length, but if you are a sprinter you should sacrifice just a tiny amount of length in order to keep your shoulders a fraction higher in the water. This, I believe, is a more powerful position even though it may not be quite as efficient.

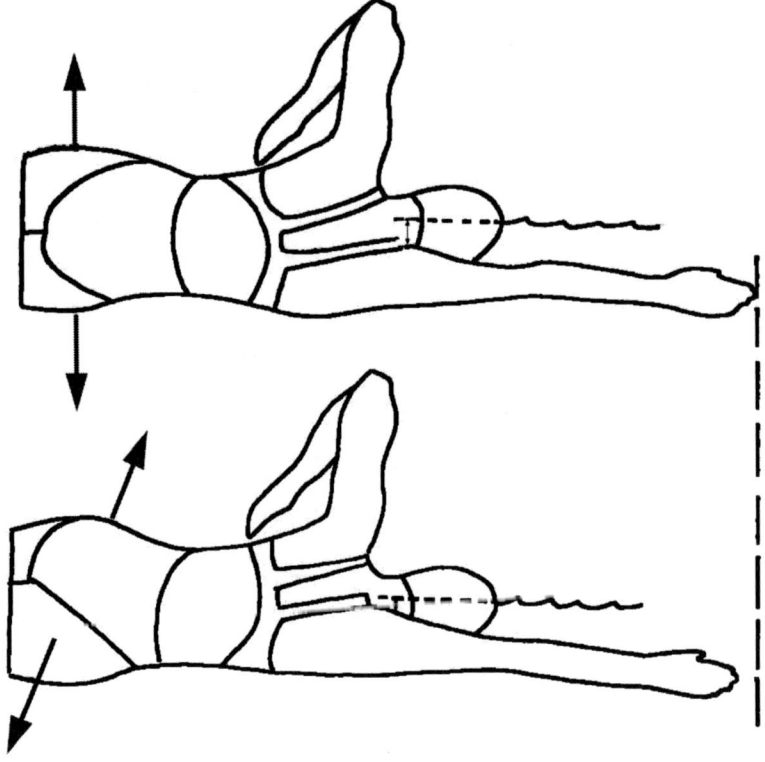

Figure 4. In the top diagram the swimmer literally turns onto their side to reach as far forwards as possible, but the shoulder is deeper than the sprinter below who sacrifices a small amount of stroke length to keep the shoulder higher.

Maybe you agree, maybe you don't. What really matters is that you understand the trade off that I'm describing and with that knowledge you experiment and decide for yourself.

Before I leave the subject of stroke length, one final small but useful point. If you tend to always breathe to one side, do check that the arm stroke on the side you don't breathe on is not too short. If, for example, you always breathe to the left, it is likely that you also always reach a good distance forwards with your right arm whether or not you actually happen to be breathing. This is because when you do breathe it has to reach a good long way to keep you balanced, and because the breath takes a bit of time you are less likely to rush into the pull. Your muscles get used to this stretch and you do it regardless of whether you are breathing or not. However, set aside some time to think about the length of your other arm stroke. If you never breathe to the right it is quite common for the stroke length of your left arm to be a touch on the short side because it is not used to being forced to stretch while you breathe.

To summarize: All freestyle swimming strokes should be long, but I believe that sprinters should be fractionally shorter than distance swimmers. This is because it allows the shoulders to remain in a higher, more powerful position.

Hip rock

The above has a consequential effect on the degree to which the hips should rock when sprinting. I have explained on page 13 that the centre of the chest should remain fairly still to avoid movement of the head. In contrast the hips should rock. As the right arm reaches forwards to take a stroke, so the right hip dips towards the bottom of the pool to allow the arm to reach further forwards. So, if you agree with my previous contention that sprinters should not reach as far forwards as they possibly can, then you should also agree that the hips of a sprinter should not dip as far as those of a distance swimmer (Figure 4). Some distance swimmers practically turn on their sides. You never see a top-level sprinter doing that.

Perhaps a more important point to make about a sprinter's hips is that they should *not* move passively. Do not be happy with the mindset that the hip moves downwards just to facilitate the arm moving further forwards. If the hip is actually driven downwards this has the effect of throwing the arm forwards. This is why I have used the title 'Upper body technique', rather than 'Arm technique' for Chapter 2.

To summarize: A sprinter's hip rock is not as pronounced as a distance swimmer's. As the hip falls it should be driven down with force and not left to drop passively.

Stroke depth

How deep should your hand and elbow be while you are pulling? Should your hand be 25 cm below you as it travels past your chest or more like 50 cm? I used to think the latter because I was oh so clever! I knew that long levers are more effective than short ones. That's why pushing a heavy door closed by the handle is easy but pushing it by the hinge is hard. It's also why I always loosen the bolts on my car tyres with the wrench handle extended. Yet again I was wrong and for the reason I refer you back to my sinking rowing boat scenario (page 21). If you submerge your whole oar deep in the water you ultimately face the problem that you have got to get it out again to take the next stroke. The time it takes you to pull your elbow back out of the deep water completely negates any extra power you get from pulling deeply. Furthermore, keeping the hand and elbow deep encourages the shoulder to drop. This leads to the chest, and ultimately head, rising and falling as I discussed earlier. So keep your hand pull quite close to your chest and make a real point of keeping your elbow bent, but definitely *high*, in the water. This way you won't get bogged down. When it's working it feels as though you are shunting the water (Figure 5).

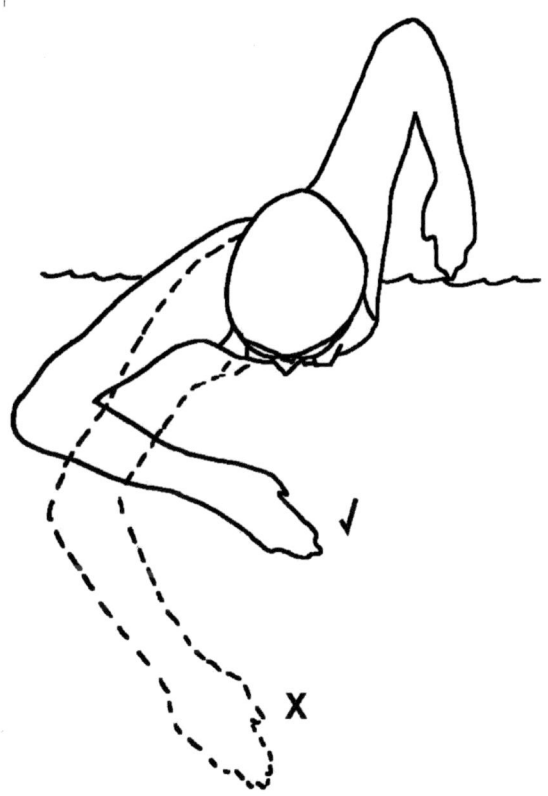

Figure 5. Keep your hand and elbow shallow in the water during the pull. It will reduce the effort involved in removing your upper arm from the water. It will also keep your shoulder high and prevent the centre of your chest from falling.

The only part of the pull that I do find it helps to deepen sometimes is the catch (that is the very beginning of the stroke when your hand catches hold of some water to pull against). I know it sounds obvious, but when you plunge your hand in do make sure you quickly get it completely under before you start pulling, otherwise you run the risk of pulling partially on surface water which is moving around and impossible to get a good grip on. This is an easy mistake to make because, in our keenness to get going, we often rush and start pulling before the hand is deep enough.

To summarize: Catch deep and pull shallow with the elbow high.

Hand entry distance

I don't know whether this works for all freestyle but I am certain it works for sprinting. Time and time again I have revived dwindling speed in my sprint sessions by remembering this. Its logic is simple. When your hand is moving forwards to take another stroke it is obviously not propelling you at all. You should therefore do whatever it takes to get it forwards as fast as possible. Why then would you slip your hand into the water early and move it forwards underneath the water which has a density 1000 times that of air? You could argue that pressing your hand down under the water helps to keep your hips and legs raised in the water behind you and thus prevents them from dragging. This may be a perfectly fair point if you have heavy, muscular legs and you struggle with this. However, during a sprint kick I find that pushing down on the water with my face and chest is sufficient to keep my legs high, so I am free to do what I like with my arms. If you do too, surely it makes more sense to move your hand forwards above the water and slip it in at the last minute. I slip it in so that it almost immediately starts to catch and pull. I'll say it again. When I am sprinting there is minimal time during which my hand is moving forwards *underneath* the water. For some reason, for me, this doesn't feel comfortable when I'm swimming at slower speeds. Perhaps a gentler kick does mean I need to push my arms down into the water to keep my legs high. The bottom line is, it's definitely worth experimenting with.

Note that I have repeatedly used the phrase 'slip it in'. If you try this, don't leave it so late that you can't put your fingers in first otherwise you will slap the water which, I'm sure you know, is a complete waste of energy. (I had a coach that occasionally made us swim a length thrashing at the water as much as possible just to remind us what a waste of time it is. It's a good idea, you get exhausted and you get nowhere).

To summarize: When sprinting minimise the time during which the hand is moving forwards *under* the water. Recover your hands over the water and then slip them in at the last minute.

4

So, what about the legs?

I'm guessing that as you've chosen to read this book you are probably a sprint freestyler yourself, or if not you coach one. My argument that your main source of propulsion, and the place to concentrate even in sprints, is your upper body could be bothering you. One of the fundamental attributes that make a sprinter is their naturally powerful leg kick. I have no doubt that your powerful legs are the reason you get away quickly off the blocks, accelerate quickly into your stroke and also get ahead off the turn. Paradoxically though, for the average club standard swimmer, a powerful leg kick can actually hinder you down the length. The reason for this is best explained by returning to my favourite analogy of hauling in a rope with a heavy weight on the end.

Imagine that you are pulling on that rope. You have it under full tension and the weight is just starting to shift towards you. Then, suddenly, somebody pushes you forwards from behind. What happens? All the tension in the rope is lost, rendering you totally helpless and unable to pull the weight towards you. You grope forwards again with the other hand to try and shorten the rope so that you can get some more tension, but somebody pushes you again and you keep groping forwards never getting the chance to make a strong effective pull on the rope. This is what happens if your leg kick in the pool is too powerful for your arms to cope with. It drives your upper body forwards so fast than your hands cannot keep a hold on the water. This is the reason why some distance swimmers, even at international level, barely kick down the length (Kieran Perkins in the Sydney Olympic 1500 m would be one example of many — have a look on YouTube). They simply find that their arms work better if they don't kick at all. They are distance swimmers; they've never liked using their legs anyway, so they just drop them completely.

So, am I actually saying that if you ease off on your legs it may make you go faster? Yes. In the short to medium term that is exactly what I am saying. I have proved it to myself time and time again. However, no one ever said this swimming business was easy! The drop off in the tempo of the legs is very *very* subtle. It only takes a tiny drop off to feel the arms strengthening and their tempo (turn over rate) immediately increases. It increases because it is easier to get them through the water when they have something to pull against. If you are kicking too hard your arms slow up because they get left in no-man's-land, just as the person hauling in the rope finds himself groping around pulling on nothing.

To actually dive in in a race, kick as hard as you can to surface as early as possible, get into your full stroke and then switch your leg kick from 100% down to 99% (while your arms stay working at 100%) is extremely difficult. Even if you have managed it in training and proved to yourself that it works, with the adrenalin flowing in a race situation it takes a lot of focus and practice. Believe me, it's hard enough in training because it is particularly hard to be working the upper part of your body as hard as possible but not the legs. It's far easier to be working everything at the same intensity. Also, as you gradually tire through your training session the balance shifts and just how hard you should be working your legs becomes a constantly moving target. Because it is so hard to do I have suggested some strategies in the training section of this book to help you learn. It is worth persevering; I knocked almost 3 seconds off my 100 m time by simply thinking 'arms arms arms' and reducing the leg tempo for the first 50 m. This experience is essentially what I was hinting at in the introduction. You may be right to have a nagging feeling that there is just something you are doing wrong but you don't know what it is. I was no fitter and no stronger than the race before. I just altered my leg tempo correctly and swam a 3 second pb.

So to the next question. If all of the above is true how come Karen Pickering practically always collapsed in her post race interviews? Her legs were so fatigued that they literally buckled underneath her? You can't tell me she didn't kick 100% the whole way through the race. Furthermore, you only have to watch the amount of splash coming from the feet of the competitors in the Olympic 50 m freestyle to realise that they are all kicking as hard as they can. So why can they do it and not us? The answer is simple. Their upper bodies and arms *are* powerful enough to cope with their strong leg kick. They are immensely powerful, but this is not the kind of power that you can get overnight. It has taken years of very hard, very specific training to get them to this point. So this is why I argued at the beginning of this book that the place to start is with the arms. If you want to greatly improve your sprint freestyle times you must make your upper body as effective and as powerful as possible and you must start today. But it will take time, and in the mean time you must learn to propel yourself with your kick at exactly the correct speed for your specific strength. And as that strength changes, so you will have to adjust your leg tempo until one day you will find that you can allow yourself to kick with 100% effort.

To summarize: **Think of your legs as an accelerator pedal. For starts and turns they should work flat out but down the length temper their pace to match your specific upper body strength. In the long-term aim to develop your upper body power so that it can cope with a flat out leg kick.**

5

Starts and turns

Starts

I know that the whole subject of track starts versus grab starts has been discussed ad infinitum, so I will keep the starts discussion short and sweet. Starts are all about stability. If you are unstable and uncomfortable on the blocks then you will never be able to respond quickly to the gun. Stability comes from flexibility. Figure 6 demonstrates that if you have extremely good flexibility in the soleus (the lowest of the calf muscles) then a grab start can give you a serious head start over your competitors. However, if you don't, then don't try it. All you'll do is wobble around trying to balance yourself and you'll either get a very slow start or you'll do a false start. In these days of the one-start rule it's just not worth the risk and that's why the track start has become so popular. But even within a group of swimmers all lined up on the blocks doing track starts, it will generally be the ones with the greatest flexibility in their hamstrings (i.e. back thighs) and calves (i.e. back of the lower legs) that get away the quickest.

The best course of action is to pick the type of start that suits your natural flexibility. Regardless of which one that is you've then got to do plenty of hamstring (page 80) and calf (page 81) stretches to make sure that you are as solid as a rock when you take your marks. Once you've settled on one, stick to it. It is the repeating of the action over and over again that brings you confidence (in fact I would advocate entering the 50 m fly or breaststroke just for starting practice). Don't keep flitting between grab starts and track starts — you'll just end up losing confidence in both.

Whichever kind of start you do, once you've left the blocks get one hand on top of the other and consciously glue them together. When the hands hit the water there is a natural tendency for them to splay apart slightly which makes you less streamlined. Make a mental note to check in training that they are still stuck together until you consciously decide to lift one off to take the first stroke.

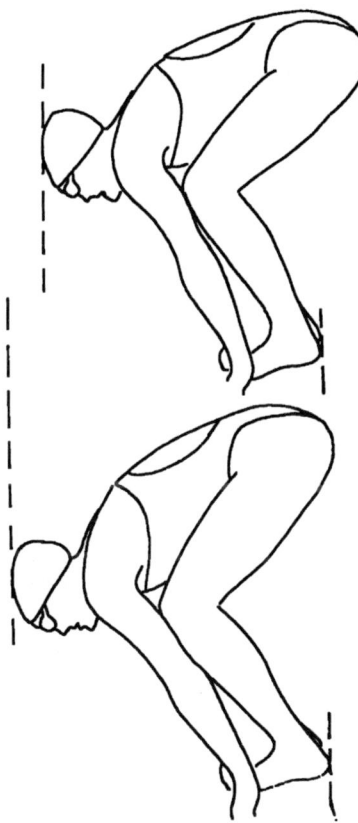

Figure 6. The swimmer at the top lacks flexibility in the soleus (the deep calf) and is already at a disadvantage before the race has even started. A lack of calf flexibility means you will have further to travel.

Turns

A tumble turn can be broken down into nine different parts all of which can be concentrated on separately.

The almighty arm pull

The secret to a good tumble turn is to convert all the horizontal speed you already have directly into rotational speed, rather than allowing it to dissipate as you drift in and over. The problem, of course, is understanding how to do it. If I was only allowed to tell you one key way to maintain the momentum you already have through a turn it would be this. Make your last pull as hard as you possibly can. Actually think to yourself 'pull hard' and whip your arm through as fast as you can. What's more, you need to learn a race stroke pattern that ensures your strongest arm is the one you turn on. Of all the points that I list in this Section, altering this alone can have a detectable impact on your time. I regularly found that, in a set of 50 m sprints, the fastest reps were when I turned on my right arm because I am right-handed. Top class hurdlers don't leave it to chance which leg they take each hurdle on and similarly you shouldn't leave it to chance which arm you turn on.

Now the chances are that you already tend to turn on the same arm anyway. It is surprising how metronomic we are. In a fresh, flat out sprint from blocks my guess is we will end up turning on the same arm nine times out of ten. So this point is probably either really good news (because you've been using your weak arm quite regularly in races) or it's of little interest because, either through luck or skill, you've been doing it anyway.

Finally, don't listen to idealistic people who tell you that instead you should strengthen your weak arm to make it as strong as your other one. That's like telling an artist with functioning hands to learn to paint with their feet — it would take years so why would they bother if their hands were perfectly good! Similarly, if you've already got a stronger arm — use it.

To summarize: Make the arm pull that takes you into the turn as strong and as fast as possible.

Chin on chest

You may never have thought of it this way, but a tumble turn is really just an upside down sit-up. Sit-ups are the traditional exercise for working your abdominal muscles (i.e. your stomach), so there is definitely an argument for doing these, or other abdominal exercises on land, as strong stomach muscles are clearly needed to execute a good turn.

Take a few seconds to lie on you back on the floor with your legs straight (not bent like a traditional sit-up because your legs are straight behind you in the pool). You will find that a single-sit up done slowly actually feels fractionally harder than one done quickly. Because of the momentum you build up when doing it quickly the last part of the fast sit-up is effortless. So, what you need in the pool is a mechanism to make you employ your stomach muscles as rapidly as you would when doing a quick sit-up on land. (On land you have the ground to push your back off, but when you are in water it's a little like being suspended in zero gravity). The way I achieve this is to physically force my chin to touch my chest. If you do it now, sitting in a chair, you should feel your stomach muscles tense up.

So, as you make your almighty pull, throw your chin onto your chest and you should feel your legs start to fly over.

To summarize: Forcing your chin onto your chest as you turn will encourage full use of your stomach muscles.

Throw the legs over

The title says it all really. Even though my previous two points should get your legs moving over quickly, it is possible to throw your legs over with force from the hips rather than just letting them drift over passively. Sometimes singling out that action in your mind, and thinking about it as you turn, makes you realise that you haven't previously been using all the strength you have. Usually its just because you've been concentrating on other things and forgotten the basics.

Foot-plant position

Most people know that you should plant your feet on the wall at either two o'clock or ten o'clock (depending on which way you prefer to turn). Most people also know the reason why. At some point in the turn you have to twist your body back onto its front otherwise you'd end up doing backstroke. It is easier to do some of that turning while you are upside down with your legs in the air. After all, air offers less resistance than water and you want to be up and into your stroke as soon as possible after you've pushed off, not adjusting the way you are facing.

I know that most people are aware of the above but I'd like to spend a little time explaining the consequences if you don't do it properly. That is if you plant your feet at one o'clock or eleven o'clock instead and leave yourself with just a bit more underwater twisting than normal. I want to go over this because you may not have put two and two together and realised that a poor foot-plant position is the cause of a common problem that I'm about to describe.

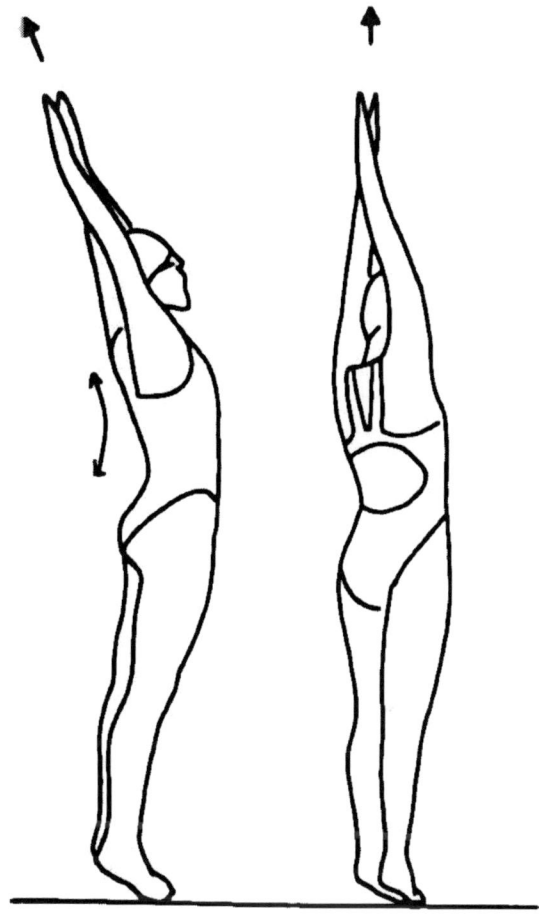

Figure 7. Looking down on the pool from the ceiling, the swimmer on the right is pushing off the wall correctly whereas the swimmer on the left has their back over arched.

When you push off the wall you should feel as though your body is a rigid arrow or a perfectly thrown javelin. The force of pushing off the wall sends you straight up in a perfect line to the surface. When it doesn't work you feel as if your upper body wasn't still and ready. Almost as if you pushed off before your upper body settled and you should have paused with your feet on the wall for a second to wait for it to catch up. But obviously you didn't because who sits around hanging on the wall in the middle of a race or a timed rep! What you actually did was what I call a 'banana turn'. You weren't like a straight javelin, you had your back over arched making your body a banana shape and consequently when you pushed off the wall your body followed the arc of the banana instead of going straight forwards (Figure 7).

The reason your body was shaped like a banana was because it was trying to twist in the water as well as surfacing, and the reason you were trying to twist in the water is because you didn't do enough twisting in the air as your feet went over.

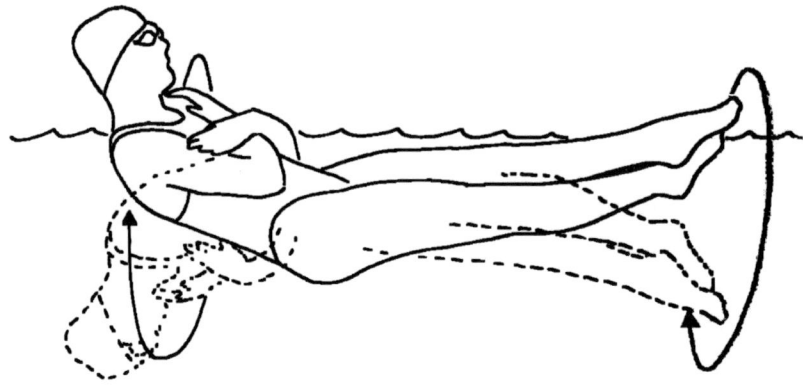

Figure 8. This exercise demonstrates that to twist your body without using your arms or legs you have to arch your back.

To demonstrate this I have a simple exercise that I used to do for fun as a child. Lie on your back in the water with your legs straight and crossed over each other and your arms also laid crossed over each other on your chest. In other words you can't use your arms or legs. Now use your core strength (i.e. move your hips, back and stomach) to twist your body round and round in the water like a corkscrew (Figure 8). As you're doing it be aware of just how much your torso is moving around to enable you to twist. Now you should be able to see why twisting in the water is never going to be compatible with moving straight forwards like an arrow.

To summarize: Plant your feet on the wall at 10 or 2 o'clock NOT 11 or 1 o'clock. If you're lazy, and don't turn as much as possible in the air, you will over arch your back as you try to finish the twist beneath the water.

Heels on the wall?

Here is a test for you. Stand up and jump up to touch the ceiling of the room you're in. What did you do? You planted your feet firmly on the ground, bent your knees and jumped. Now do the same but this time you're not allowed to touch the ground with your heels. You have to do it all balancing on the balls of your feet. Did you do as well? I'm guessing you jumped about the same height, but it took you twice as long because you wobbled around keeping your balance while you bent your knees. The effect is less pronounced when you're pushing off the wall in a tumble turn because the water supports your weight and you don't have to struggle to balance as much, but I suspect you do have to balance yourself a bit. So try experimenting with landing your heels onto the wall with your legs bent at the correct angle to go straight into what is effectively a squat jump. It is with this in mind that you should work out how far from the wall to start your turn. Don't turn so far out that your legs end up straight and you have to sink backwards because that wastes time.

Note that if you have very tight deep calf muscles (the back of your lower leg) you'll probably find that you don't manage to get your heels on the wall. The way to test your flexibility here is to try to squat the way the Chinese do to play Mah-jong. If you can't do it your turns could benefit from stretching or some sports massage (page 81).

To summarize: Try getting your heels onto the wall when you turn and see whether it speeds up your push off the wall.

Head tucked

Tucking your head in makes you more streamlined, so don't just tuck it in a little, tuck it in a lot. Bury it right beneath your arms.

Surface quickly

When you have pushed off the wall your body immediately starts slowing down due to friction between it and the water. For each of the four strokes there is therefore a point in time when the speed of your glide has slowed down to exactly the same speed as your full stroke. Ideally fractionally before this point you should prepare yourself to surface and start swimming so that the transition between the two is perfect. There should never be a point when you glide slower than you can swim. When it works you know it; it's a bit like changing gear in the car at exactly the right speed. The transition is so smooth you hardly notice it has been done. As a freestyle sprint is the fastest of all the strokes you should spend the least amount of time underwater gliding off the turn (or off the start for that matter) because this 'perfect point' occurs sooner.

Those who successfully do fly kick off the wall are effectively prolonging the initial higher speeds of the glide before they surface. This is fine to do if you have a strong fly kick but there's no point doing it if you don't. So if you're deliberating about whether or not to do fly kick off the wall this knowledge about what it's actually doing may help you decide. If you have a relatively weak fly kick I wouldn't bother. Theoretically there is a point, when you are changing from fly kick to freestyle kick, at which you have an in-between, and very ineffectual kick indeed, and that can be avoided if you go straight into freestyle kick off the turn.

To summarize: Because sprint freestyle is the fastest stroke the time it takes to surface should be short. If you have a weak kick, get up quick!

Use your hands as rudders

If you find that you are a little late surfacing try using your hands as rudders. One hand should always be on top of the other as you surface so just tilt both hands at the wrist, so that your fingers are pointing up towards the ceiling, and you'll find your body soon follows.

Stroke on the lowest hip side

This tip comes from an Olympic medallist and, after she'd pointed it out, boy did I feel stupid!

After a tumble turn everybody pushes off the wall with one hip dipping down towards the bottom of the pool. If you turn at two o'clock (i.e. with your legs to the right) then you will come out on your right side with your right hip nearer to the bottom of the pool, and vice versa. So following on from the discussion on page 23 about how the hip dips to enable a longer stroke length, why on earth would you ever turn to the right, push off with your right hip dipping down, straighten up and then take your first stroke with your left arm? Surely, as your body is set up with the right hip dipped anyway, you should take your first stroke with your right arm. It's crazy not to.

If you're not already doing this the implications are huge because it transforms you from a swimmer that typically breathes on the first stroke after surfacing into one that breathes on the third stroke after surfacing. And that, in turn, knocks socks off your time because you speed up much more quickly if your body is streamlined (i.e. not trying to take a breath). It's far better to wait until you're into your stroke rhythm before you breathe. Using this method you get into your stroke and surface so much more quickly that you can easily hold your breath for long enough.

To summarize: Take your first stroke on the side that you've just turned on.

6
Breathing

Breathing in swimming is a true catch-22. I mentioned earlier that the golden rule of all sports is to keep the head still. If your head is rocking around your brain has no hope of putting all your appendages in the right places (Figure 2, page 14). The catch-22 of freestyle is that the best place to put your face is perfectly still and in the water, but you can't breathe underwater and you need to breathe to refuel your body. So you have to move your head, which in turn slows you down and, once you've slowed down, you need more energy to speed up again, which requires more breathing — and so it goes on in a negative spiral!

The solution is twofold. Firstly you minimise the movement of the head during the breathing action and secondly you breathe as little as possible.

To understand just how little the head needs to move try this simple demonstration. Standing in the shallow end of the pool, hold your hand up vertically so that your fingers are above the water pointing to the ceiling and the palm of your hand is beneath the water. Now push forwards against the water and you will see that immediately behind your hand the water surface is lower than the rest of the pool. As long as your hand is moving forwards this dip in the surface is always there. When you head is moving forwards through the water it has the same effect. It creates a dip in the surface behind it. This means that you do not actually have to lift your head at all to breathe. The Total Immersion* drills demonstrate just how devastating the effect of lifting your head is upon your legs, which will immediately drop and act as a brake. So it is a relief to realise that you don't ever need to. In actual fact the movement of the head to breath is a twisting action and not a lifting action at all, and the way to learn it is to play a little game. You have to pretend that your head is stuck to your shoulder. You are allowed to change the part of your head that is touching the shoulder but you are never allowed to take it off. So you start with your ear touching it and as you roll your head around to breathe you end up with the very back of your head touching it. It feels a little weird at first, but it soon becomes second nature.

The distance swimmers' solution to reducing the number of breaths is to breathe bilaterally (that is every three strokes and thus on opposites sides). Not only does this reduce the number of breaths they take, but it also balances their stroke reducing the risk of a repetitive strain injury. I speak from personal experience here as I once had a pain in my side for months caused by doing long swims breathing on one side only. Once I had it, it was really hard to shift. Sprinters obviously need to be fit and there is a place for aerobic sessions in their training (see Part II) so bilateral breathing is a skill they need and should be worked on away from the racing season. However, that is all they need; to breathe every three strokes so that they can keep fit without injury. They do not need to be doing sets of 100 m swims, off very little rest, breathing every 3 strokes, 5 strokes, 7 strokes etc. Whether these help the distance swimmers or not I could not comment, but I do not think they help a

---

Total Immersion. The Revolutionary way to swim better, faster and easier. 1997 and 2004. Terry Laughlin with John Delves. Simon and Schuster

sprinter reduce the number of breaths they take over the course of a 50 m sprint.

So what do sprinters need to do? How often do you hear someone say 'And did you see the guy who won the 50 m freestyle — he didn't even breathe once'. To sprint 50 m without breathing is truly impressive, and something to aspire to, but the important message here is if you can't do it, don't do it.

Let's talk common sense and hope it prevails! Most swimmers can sprint 25 m of freestyle without breathing and there is no doubt in my mind that, all other things being equal, you will swim 25 m faster if you don't breathe than if you do. The time it takes to take that breath is not compensated for by the energy derived from the extra oxygen you take in. I have proved this to myself over and over again in training. However, this cannot go on indefinitely. If one kept sprinting down a pool of infinite length there would come a point where the body would come to a complete standstill. You would either pass out or take a breath. Your decline in speed to reach this point would not be instantaneous either. It may not be perfectly linear, but it would be graduated in some way as all the available energy production systems became depleted.

It seems logical to me that at some point between just beyond the 25 m mark and this 'standstill' mark there is a stretch of water, any point in which, you would have got to quicker had you taken a breath. Furthermore, at the beginning of this stretch of water is a single point where it makes no difference whether you'd taken a breath earlier or not. The extra energy you got from the oxygen you took in during the breath, despite the time it took, would exactly balance out the decline in speed you experienced if you didn't breathe before you got to it. The exact location of this point, in metres varies (and I suspect hugely) from person to person. I am certain that through the correct training an individual can extend this point and so diminish the number of breaths they take in a race, but I am equally certain that if everyone in a squad tries to sprint 50 m tomorrow without breathing at all, many of them will not go faster.

The philosophy that everyone in the squad should therefore swim until they are bursting to take a breath, and then take one if they have to, cannot be relied upon because they should have taken that breath several strokes earlier. By the time you are bursting it is too late. You need to anticipate the need to breath and you can only do that by identifying, and then experimenting with, your current breathing pattern in training. Once you have established where your breaths currently are you can begin to move them further back as you become faster.

A good place to start is to get someone to time you, off blocks, to the 30 m mark in a 25 m pool (i.e. the end of the 5 m mark as you come out of the turn). Can you get there quicker with or without a breath on the way up? Personally, if I didn't breathe a few strokes before the turn I never could make the turn powerful enough to get there quicker. (Never breathe just before a turn, always a few strokes out so that you can be at full speed going into the turn).

A few words of warning before I leave this subject. Firstly, just because you can just about manage a breathing pattern in the first rep of training doesn't always mean you can do it in a race. Due to pre-race nerves your heart rate is slightly higher than it is before the first rep of your training session.

Finally, and probably of equal importance to anything else in this section so far; if you've ever experienced a feeling of weakness as you surface off your dive in a race, it is probably due to the fact that you were holding your breath before the start of the race without realising it. For some bizarre reason humans hold their breath when they are nervous about anything and this includes nerves before a race. If you concentrate on one thing before you get on the blocks it should be to keep breathing right there and then, otherwise you'll be heading towards an oxygen debt before you've even started!

To summarize: Glue your head to your shoulder; learn your race breathing pattern and then gradually extend it and if you are nervous think — breathe!

Part II
Training

7

The complete tool kit

The first part of this book has essentially been a discussion of some technical aspects of sprinting freestyle. But technical ability is only one of the skills that a sprint swimmer needs to be successful. In Part II I identify the 'tools' needed to complete your sprinting 'tool kit' and then develop an understanding of how to acquire them. In other words, I will explain what training I think needs to be done, why it needs to be done and when it needs to be done.

So, here is my complete list of skills. Some of them need more detail than is given here so I have dedicated additional Sections to them later on. I make no apologies for fitting them into an imaginary timetable. This serves to demonstrate how short time is and how the function and goals of every session must be clearly understood.

Rest

I bet you didn't think this would be first on the list? The ability to identify when you need a rest is a crucial skill that only comes with experience. It takes considerable self-will to be able to override the fear of 'getting behind' with the understanding that doing the training will do more harm than good if you have not fully recovered from the previous session (Figure 9). One way to monitor the need for a rest is to consistently monitor the times of all your training swims (page

60), but without doubt one day each week should be set aside for total mental and physical rest and in my ideal week this is a Friday because most people feel exhausted by work or school by Friday. An additional rest day should be taken once every 3 to 4 weeks. Sprint training is about quality not quantity.

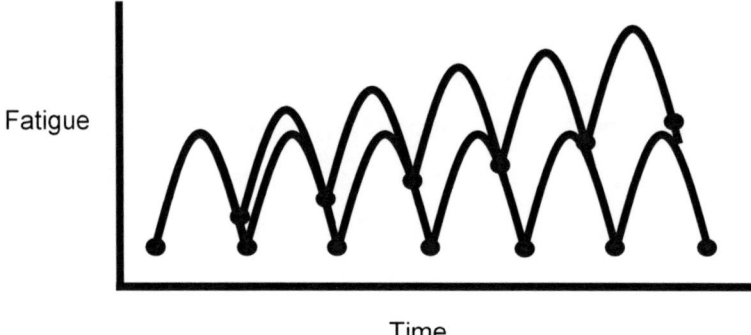

Figure 9. A theoretical demonstration of the effect of repeatedly training before the body has fully recovered. Each black dot represents a training session. The swimmer following the top line may eventually cram an extra session in, but at what cost?

The most important rest we can have is sleep. Whether it's a glass of wine, a snack or a warm bath before bed, work out what you need to get a good night's sleep. One of the most common causes of struggling to sleep is tension in the upper back and neck so I have included an excellent yoga position on page 84 that helps eliminate this.

	Prelim. set	Main set
Mon		
Tue		
Wed		
Thru		
Fri	----------------Complete rest----------------	
Sat		
Sun		

Speed

It may seem a bit confusing to set aside this as one skill alone. Isn't speed just another word for sprint and hence the overall aim of the book anyway? Well, yes it is, and consequently some of the other skills on this list obviously contribute to improvements in your speed. More specifically the skill sought here is cadence (which is the posh word for 'arm turnover rate'). Thus these sessions train your muscles to do the correct action faster[*].

The ethos is quite simple. You will never increase your maximum speed if you don't swim at your current maximum speed on a regular basis. By 'maximum speed' I don't mean your speed over a given distance, I mean your completely fresh top speed that you can achieve only for a short period of time. You may have heard of top swimmers being dragged along by machines, which pull them fractionally faster than they can swim, in order to increase their top speed. Those of us that don't have access to such a machine have to settle for our self propelled maximum speed. To achieve that you need to take significant rests between each training rep, and within each rep you need to fatigue as little as possible otherwise you will just end up compromising your stroke. So these swims need to be as short as possible — mine were always only 25 m (but less would be better if you have access to a shorter pool) and the rest should never be less than 2 to 3 minutes and frequently far more. You may need to swim extremely gently in-between reps to stop yourself

---

[*] I once tried to estimate how many strokes the top swimmers take per second. I wanted to set my countdown repeat watch to bleep each time I should be taking a stroke. I reckoned on about 1½ strokes per second. Unfortunately my watch wasn't clever enough to bleep every 0.66 of a second but it's worth a try if you have the technology.

getting cold and towards the racing season, when you have greater rest, get out and towel down, as you would at a competition, and do them off blocks.

These sessions are the real opportunity to experiment with all the technical points I raised in the Part I. Particularly though, they are an excellent opportunity to experiment with varying the leg tempo. I often found that I could increase my speed by dropping off my leg tempo after a preset number of strokes down the length.

These speed sessions are the highest quality session there is so always try to do them the day after a rest day.

	Prelim. set	Main set
Mon		
Tue		
Wed		
Thur		
Fri	----------------Complete rest----------------	
Sat		Sprints
Sun		

Fitness and weight maintenance

Even if you are a 50 m sprinter an aerobic session (where the heart rate is raised to a moderate level for a prolonged period of time), once a week, is necessary for two reasons.

Firstly, success in sprinting is heavily dependent on your power to weight ratio. The higher this is the better. Just like any fraction it can be raised by either increasing the numerator (your power) or by reducing the denominator (your weight). Either way you go faster. For example, you could be no more powerful at all, but if you loose half a kilo you will go faster. To understand how much faster, turn this scenario on its head and imagine how much slower you'd be if you strapped half a kilo to your back and then tried to sprint even 25 m? So these are the sessions that help you loose a little weight if you need to, and maintain your low weight if/once you're at the right level.

Secondly, you have to be fit enough to get through all your other training sessions. If you do a set of fairly demanding stroke drills before your main training set, you have to be able to completely recover from them before starting the main set.

I believe that it is far better to do these aerobic sessions out of the pool — that is to 'cross-train'. This is a bit of a break with tradition but it makes sense when you consider my initial point in Part II about the constant need for complete recovery. Part I of this book emphasised that the majority of energy required in swimming is channelled through the upper body. But it doesn't matter what you do for a fitness session as long as you raise your heart rate so doesn't it make sense to do a sport that uses your legs so that your arms can have an extra day of rest and be properly recovered ready for the next pool session? I would advocate doing a 30 to 40 minute run, bike ride, football match or anything else that you enjoy. You don't need to worry that building up the wrong muscle sets might affect your weight distribution in the pool either. Marathon runners don't have big muscles, only sprint runners do, so as long as you avoid another form of sprinting you'll be fine.

Following on from this, it's important that coaches take on board what teenagers are doing as extra-curricular school sports. If a school child has a sports match that goes into extra time on a Saturday afternoon, don't ask them do an aerobic pool set the next day. There's no point, they've done it already!

As the fitness session buys time for arm recovery, it should be slotted in between heavy pool sessions. In my ideal week I have therefore put it on Sunday; the day after the high quality sprint session and the day before the next high quality swimming session — lactate tolerance. (This also means that if you are away for a weekend, you don't have to find a pool to train in — you can go for a run anywhere).

	Prelim. set	Main set
Mon		
Tue		
Wed		
Thur		
Fri	----------------Complete rest----------------	
Sat		Sprints
Sun	Aerobic	

Lactate tolerance (and a race strategy)

In this day and age most people involved in sport have heard of lactic acid. It is a compound that is formed when the oxygen we breathe in is being used up a faster rate than we can replenish it. Once lactic acid starts to build up in the muscles (after approximately 15 to 20 seconds of intense exertion) it rapidly becomes crippling. To help you understand the nature of the beast it may help to know that plants produce a very similar compound when confronted with the same situation — it's called alcohol! To state that lactic acid build up is like making your muscles drunk is probably getting away from scientific accuracy, but it helps to get the general message across that in large quantities this is a toxin. Translated into swimmer's English, lactic acid is the stuff that makes your arms and legs feel like lead weights in the final few metres of your race. This crippling is infact a mechanism which evolution has perfected over several million years to stop us over exercising and thus prevent us from poisoning ourselves to death (the yeast do die when we brew alcohol). So how do we beat it? Well, for the reasons I've just described, it would be very dangerous to beat it completely even if we could. However, lactic acid is not entirely a waste product. It is something of a by-product in that once it has been generated it too can be broken down and used for energy production (though not nearly as efficiently as aerobic respiration). So lactic acid can be removed and reprocessed and it turns out that we can train our bodies to do this more efficiently. This is what lactic tolerance training is all about. The million dollar question is how? Well, if you're going to get better at reprocessing it, you've got to generate it, and that means swimming pretty fast for distances further than your race. Generally speaking reps within a lactic session will involve 75, 100, 125 and 150 m swims all at around about only 12% slower than race pace would be for each of them. As with sprint sessions, you do therefore have to have enough rest to get your breath back and lower your heart rate, but unlike sprint sessions you have to swim a lot further in between the rests! If you are not confident that you are doing lactic tolerance sets correctly there's one sure way to tell. It's not pleasant, but for reasons that you'll now understand, it often makes you feel slightly sick.

Race strategy

In keeping with the general message of this book, I do these lactate session arms-only for most, but not quite all, of the year. It is sufficient to do lactic tolerance training for the first 7 to 8 months. After that you are not really going to make much more difference and the time is better spent moving on to thinking about a race strategy. For this reason, from approximately month six to month eight, phase the lactic sets down until they become sets of arms-only 50 m swims (or 100 m if that's your race distance) off blocks. This session then becomes the basis for experimenting with race kicking and breathing patterns as the major competitions approach. Spend a few weeks eking out as much speed as you can on these arms-only swims and, when you feel you can go no faster, allow yourself to bring in your legs for limited periods. For example, allow yourself to kick out of the turn and see how much faster you can go. Then allow yourself to kick out of the dive also. Perhaps then add in kick in the last 10 m etc. The aim is to see if you can beat last year's training times for full stroke before you reach full stroke this year. It gives a real psychological boost to know that you've gone faster than you did last year without even using your legs down the middle of the first length because the next natural thought is — think what I can do full stroke now!

After you've got the kick where you want it, start to analyse and then shift your breathing pattern as explained on page 45. By the time your biggest race arrives these sessions have become pure race practice e.g. 3 x 50 m off blocks with 15 minutes rest during which you towel down.

In the off-season these are always tough sessions and throughout the year they are high quality, so I have place them second of the pool sessions in the week, after sprints. Your arms should still be fairly fresh having had a complete rest the day before if you follow my recommendation of cross-training for the aerobic session.

	Prelim. set	Main set
Mon		Lactate tolerance
Tue		
Wed		
Thur		
Fri	---------------Complete rest---------------	
Sat		Sprints
Sun		Aerobic

Power

In the first part of this book I explained why sprint freestyle swimmers should aspire to have upper bodies that are powerful enough to cope with the propulsive force of their legs (page 28). Because training for power development in the upper body and other areas requires a fairly lengthy discussion, I have dedicated a separate Chapter to it later on in the book. I explain there why I have allocated both land and pool sessions each week to power. For now though, it just needs to be noted as an important skill and allocated its slots in the timetable. Note that at least two nights rest are allowed in-between power sessions to allow the muscles to fully repair themselves.

	Prelim. set	Main set
Mon		Lactate tolerance
Tue		Power weights
Wed		
Thur		Power in the pool
Fri	----------------Complete rest----------------	
Sat		Sprints
Sun		Aerobic

Choice and enjoyment

Any training regime needs to be flexible. There will often be periods when you feel a particular aspect of training is not going well and, whether this perceived or genuine, the 'Choice' session is there to help you get on with it and get over it. E.g. Pure 50 m sprinters may feel the need for an additional speed session whereas those more inclined towards the 100 m may benefit from another lactic tolerance or aerobic session. The only thing I would say is don't make it a Power session unless you do a lot of juggling with the weekly timetable. To do three Power sessions in a row is not advisable.

It's also there for Enjoyment too. Sometimes it's easy to get bogged down with training and forget to swim purely because its what you love to do. If you enjoy other strokes then do them (Fly is particularly complementary to freestyle). Equally, if you need a break then you can take it and do something else with your life without worrying that you are getting behind.

In the racing season, however, Choice should definitely be a rest. That way you can have a rest on Wednesday and Friday, do a high quality sprint session in between on Thursday, and you'll be fresh and ready for a race at the weekend.

	Prelim. set	Main set
Mon		Lactate tolerance
Tue		Power weights
Wed		Choice
Thur		Power in the pool
Fri	----------------Complete rest----------------	
Sat		Sprints
Sun		Aerobic

Technique and flexibility

These are the sessions in which you develop and maintain your technical ability. In the pool this means concentrating on your stroke and turn execution and out of the pool it means working on flexibility to enable you to physically achieve the pool work.

Flexibility needs to be worked on regularly. I have dedicated a later Chapter to this in which it is recommend five days out of seven, directly after the main exercise of the day. Which five days don't really matter too much but make sure you definitely do some after weight training and do not do any on your rest day. Weekends are good because there tends to be more time available.

The complete toolkit

A short set of swims, concentrating purely on technique, should be done after the warm up and before the main training set (here called the Prelim. set). I separate them into two types — a 'turn' set (Appendix A) and a 'stroke' set (Appendix B). I don't really like to call them drills. Whilst a few involve a slight alteration of the stroke, the majority are just concentration exercises designed to start with the basics and build up to a powerful, top quality tumble turn or sprint stroke respectively.

I put the tumble turn set before the lactic session simply because you do a lot of fast turns in these so it is an opportunity for the correct action to be drilled into the subconscious.

	Prelim. set	Main set	Post set
Mon	Warm-up + turn technique	Lactate tolerance	Flexibility
Tue		Power weights	Flexibility
Wed	(Warm-up + stroke technique*)	Choice	
Thur	Warm-up + stroke technique	Power in the pool	Flexibility
Fri	----------------------------------Complete rest----------------------------------		
Sat	Warm-up + stroke technique	Sprints	Flexibility
Sun		Aerobic	Flexibility

*When Choice is a pool session

8
Time monitoring

Unless you have someone who can come to your training sessions, and be fully attentive to the majority of your swims, then you should get into the habit of timing yourself. For sprint training the pool clock is not accurate enough. You need to know and record your time to the nearest tenth of a second. It's not that difficult to do. Just wear a waterproof watch with a stopwatch function. The time does not have to be the absolute correct time. If there is an error it doesn't matter as long as it is a fairly consistent error, i.e. it will always take you about the same fraction of a second to bring your finger to the off button. You soon get used to it and develop a regular method. Plus, if you get a watch with an automatic start function (which usually comes with watches that have a countdown repeat function) then it can give you a few get ready bleeps and a go bleep which means you don't encounter an error in starting it. This is great because it means you can time yourself off blocks. You just start it and then have 5 or 6 seconds to get in position. It's a bit like a delayed action button on a camera.

A soft pencil will not rip a piece of wet paper and it doesn't matter if a pencil gets wet so it's easy to record your times from inside the pool.

So, why should you bother? Here are just a few reasons:

You won't learn anything if you don't

The reason I have been able to write this book is that I timed virtually every single 25 m sprint I did in a period of about 8 years. I dread to think how many that is, but it means that I gradually learned what works and what doesn't. You can't learn instantaneously. It takes time because there is always the question — was that slower because I changed something technical or was it because I tired? However, over a period of a few months patterns begin to emerge and you'll realise that, on average, you're faster if you try one thing instead of another. For example, did you know that on average you will swim a 25 m sprint faster if you start at the deep end rather than the shallow end? The difference is miniscule, but it is definitely there; presumably because your body is less affected by the friction between the water and the bottom of the pool when trying to accelerate at the deep end.

Of all the sports, swimming is perhaps the most dependent on the stopwatch for learning purposes. When we are travelling in a car or running along a road we can detect small alterations in our speed by observing how quickly the objects around us pass out of view. But with your head under the water you have no reference point, so minor changes in speed are hard to spot. Because swimmers can't observe any changes in the instant that they happen, but have to wait until the end of a rep to look at the stopwatch, it makes what we might call 'responsive learning' very difficult. Cause and effect become very difficult to detect. The only solution is to focus on one specific technical point at a time and to time everything.

Have I warmed up properly?

In a similar vain to above. Is the first rep of your main set always your fastest? OK, often you might specifically intend it not to be for the purposes of the training session, but if it should be equal in time to all the others, is it? Because this first rep is equivalent to your race. It's no good always swimming a bit better on the second or third rep. You don't get a second chance in a race. If you do find this then you know you have not warmed up properly and can do something about it. If of course you always just use the pool clock, you may not even notice as much as half a second!

Am I ill? Should I train?

Everybody has this dilemma from time to time. You feel a bit under the weather and you're not sure whether to train or not. If you are in the habit of timing yourself then the watch will make the decision for you. You'll have a good idea before you start the session what sort of time you should be achieving comfortably and if, after a few reps, you are clearly not achieving it then you know its time to stop. The beauty of this is that it means you don't complete the session and end up making yourself really ill.

It gives a psychological incentive.

If you follow a fairly normal training year then the early off-season swims will tend to be higher volume with less rest than when you are approaching the racing season. It helps to know your times because when you get a swim technically right you can often get a surprisingly good time even though you are heavily fatigued. Knowing the result can make you think — 'If I can do that now just think what I'll be able to do in a few months with more rest beforehand'. It gives self-belief which is really important. In this way the whole training year can become an ongoing competition with yourself which is both fun and inspirational. I used to keep a log of what I called my 'training pbs' and it felt good beating them.

9
Training for power

What is power?

Before we look at how to achieve it, it is useful to clarify the meaning of the word *power*. What is the difference between power and strength? Put simply, a strong person may be able to move a heavy weight from point A to point B, but a *powerful* person can move it from A to B quickly. A powerful person is not just strong. A powerful person can apply their strength with speed — that is, with explosive force.

So, first of all, how do you get more strength? You make your muscles work against a weight that will resist the force they are applying. In doing this work your muscles actually get damaged but only on a micro scale. Due to the strain the muscles get tiny tears (all the way along their length if you're doing it properly) and when the body repairs these micro-tears it repairs them slightly stronger than they were before. Thus, repeated resistance training over a prolonged period of time, but with enough rest between individual sessions to allow the body to repair the muscles, leads to increased strength.

So how do you get more powerful? You do resistance training but each time you ask your muscles to work against the resisting force you do it explosively (with the obvious confine that you do it sensibly so that you don't injure yourself).

Training for power

Current thinking with regards to resistance training is that you should be performing each exercise with a weight that you can only manage about 10 to 15 times. If you can do the exercise more than this you will just get fitter and a little more powerful on the side.

In the pool or on land?

With the above in mind, let's look at an example of a resistance exercise that is useful to swimmers and leads us conveniently on to the next consideration — whether we should do resistance training in the pool or on land. The exercise we'll consider is squats. For these you stand with your legs shoulder width apart, toes pointing slightly outwards. Both knees are then bent at the same time until they are at about 90 degrees so that your upper legs are parallel to the floor (or more if you are flexible enough). You then use your quads (your front thighs) to push yourself up to a standing position again (Figure 10). If you are a swimmer this is an action that you do every time you push off the wall so the more powerfully you can do it the better.

I'm sure you can imagine that if you were asked to do Squats with just the resistance of water pushing against you, you would be able to do far more than 10 to 15 in a row before you got tired. (For example, you could do far more than 15 tumble turns swimming back and forth across the width of a small pool). For this reason, to *strengthen* the quads, we can come out of the pool and do Squats with a barbell held across the back of our shoulders (Figure 10), gradually increasing the weight until we reach a level where we can only do it in sets of 10 to 15 lifts. Following on from this and the discussion above, to develop *power* in the quads we can lower the weight on our shoulders but, instead of just straightening the legs, we actually aim to jump as high as we can still holding some weight across the back of our shoulders. This is an explosive action and therefore develops power as opposed to just strength.

Figure 10. The position for Squats

Bending at the knees and jumping (a Squat jump) is a fairly simple action. It is easy to visualise that it is the same action as the legs do in a turn or a dive, but just translated across to land. Consider though the arm pulling action in freestyle, which involves a plethora of muscles from the wrist right down to the stomach. We can try to do weight training on land either by isolating the major muscle groups involved or by replicating the whole action, and we should try because we will never be able to generate as much resistance in the pool as we can through weight training. However, no exercise will ever encompass all the muscles involved. So for all-round power training we have to accept the old adage that 'there is no substitute for the real thing' and also do power training in the pool, working with the best resistance that we can.

Areas to concentrate

So many books get carried away in the power Section and seem to be a compilation of every single exercise ever developed. In actual fact, with a little thought, those needed to cover 90% of your swimming power can be narrowed down to a small group that can have a real effect on your time. If you've never done weights before you do need to get advice from someone qualified to teach you. If you don't do it properly you run the risk of injury, particularly to your back, which gets you nowhere fast. The website www.momentumsports.co.uk is also a useful reference. It's a website for runners but it is full of video clips of both power and flexibility exercises. All I will do here is explain the exercises. There are all sorts of issues, such as at what age children should be allowed to do it and whether to wear a weights belt or not, that I am not qualified to answer. It goes without saying though, that you should be properly warmed up before you start (page 76).

Working systematically through Part I reveals that power exercises need to be developed for the following (in diminishing order of importance):

- Driving the arm recovery above the water
- The upper body underwater pull (and push at the end)
- The stomach for turns and generally maintaining posture
- The hips so that they can be driven downwards rather than drifting
- The front thigh (quads) for starts and turns

Driving the arm recovery

If the underwater pulling action in freestyle involves a multitude of muscles from your wrist to your biceps (forearms) to your stomach, why then do the tops of the backs of your arms (your deltoids) burn and tighten after a hard session? After exercise that demands a multitude of muscles, such as the swimming pull, the body's response is one of intense, general fatigue, presumably because large amounts of glycogen (energy stores) have been used up all over the body. But this pain in the back of a swimmer's arms is different. It is, as I have said, a burning sensation. The kind of pain one gets when a single small set of muscles has been repeatedly used, virtually on its own. This burning sensation is not caused by pulling but by the repeated action of driving the elbow back out of the water, holding it high and throwing it forwards through the air. In other words the arm recovery action. The power demand that this places on a limited number of muscles (mainly the deltoids) is, I believe, a major limiting factor to the speed of most sprint freestyle swimmers. The sprinter that has powerful deltoids can achieve a high cadence (arm turnover rate) without compromising stroke length, which leads in turn to sprinting success.

So how do you get powerful deltoids?

On land

Simply mimic the action and you have the fairly standard weight lifting exercise shown in Figure 11. The usual provisos apply — make sure your back is straight and the weight is sensible.

In the pool

The age-old quandary about power training in the pool is how best to create the required resistance? In an ideal world we would just swim

Training for power

through glue but that is clearly not possible. Many people turn to paddles for this but I do not recommend them. My reasoning is that paddles create a resistance to pulling underwater, but not to the arm recovery. The consequence is that the swimmer ends up taking an almighty pull (which is good) but then they have to get a huge paddle out of the water (finger paddles would not give enough resistance). The temptation is to languish around with their arms in the air as if there is all the time in the world having a rest. With hand paddles there is no incentive to get the arms forward quickly and you need something that provides this. Paddles have their place in improving technical awareness in the underwater pull but they are not the best aid to power development.

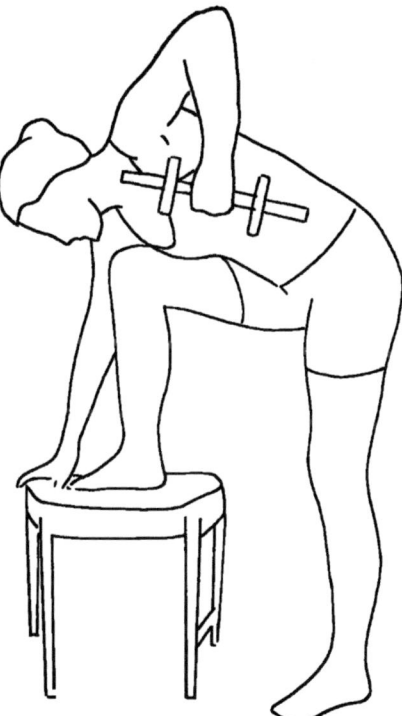

Figure 11. The deltoid lift

What is needed then is something that provides a constant resistance so that the momentum generated from the pull is limited slightly and the swimmer is encouraged to throw their arms forwards to stop themselves coming to a standstill. This should preferably be something that doesn't interfere with the stroke. Umbrellas are available which are fastened around the waist and drag like a net behind you. The problem with these is that although they provide constant resistance down the length, they do not around the turn. They stop and then suddenly yank you back after you've pushed off the wall. Plus, there is a tendency to get tangled up in the cord as you turn.

The best solution is a drag belt worn around the hips with detachable cups, or some other system, that can be used to vary the resistance so that it is correct for the individual. Because the belt is low and close to the hips it does not interfere with the stroke and it gives a consistent resistance throughout the swim. I combine this with a large rubber band (made by cutting the top off an old swim hat) around the legs, which completely stops me from kicking down the length, and thus allows for time comparisons throughout the year. The beauty of it is that you can still do fly kick off the wall which stops you coming to a complete standstill of each turn and keeps the work rate constant.

With regards to the nature of the reps, if we assume that you will take around about 18 to 20 strokes in 25 m then each arm does 9 to 10 pulls down the length of a short course pool. So, following on from the 'not more than 10 to 15 reps' rule, you should definitely not do more than 50 m. It is *crucial* that if 50 m feels too easy the resistance is increased and not the distance covered. The only exception to this might be at the very beginning of the training year, when the main focus is on fitness, and you are perhaps not used to using drag aids so might benefit from longer, lower resistance swims.

During these sets concentrate on finishing the pull quickly and driving the elbow out of the water.

The underwater pull

On land

I tried and tried to separate all the muscles that are involved in the freestyle pull and then to exercise them individually, but for various reasons I never really found it satisfactory. My solution is the poor man's swim bench. As promised on page 12 I have written it up below as an introductory exercise to demonstrate why the centre line of the body is the correct pulling path to follow, but once you've done this just adjust the weight and develop it into a proper power training set.

You need: a pulley with an eye in it (which you can get cheaply from a DIY shop), some rope, a series of weights ranging from about 5 to 20 kg and a pair of gloves (weights or cycling gloves are great). Thread a piece of rope through the eye of the pulley and suspend it somewhere where there is plenty of space around it. I used to use the rafters in the garage, but a strong tree branch would do. It needs to be higher than the height you can reach with your hand extended above your head. Tie a weight (about 8 to 12 kg to start with) to one end of another piece of rope and place it beneath the pulley. Stand on a chair and thread the other end of the rope around the pulley wheel. Move the chair away, put your gloves on and, standing directly in front of the weights but on the other side of the pulley, pull the rope until there is tension on it but the weights remain still on the ground still on the other side. Reach your strongest arm up as high as you comfortably can and wrap the rope around your hand a few times to secure it. Keeping your back straight, aim to raise the weights off the ground the other side by pulling your hand down along the centre line of your body. Do this a few times with a view to finding the maximum weight you can manage comfortably. Don't push yourself to hard if you've never done it before, you will just end up injuring yourself and this is only a demonstration exercise.

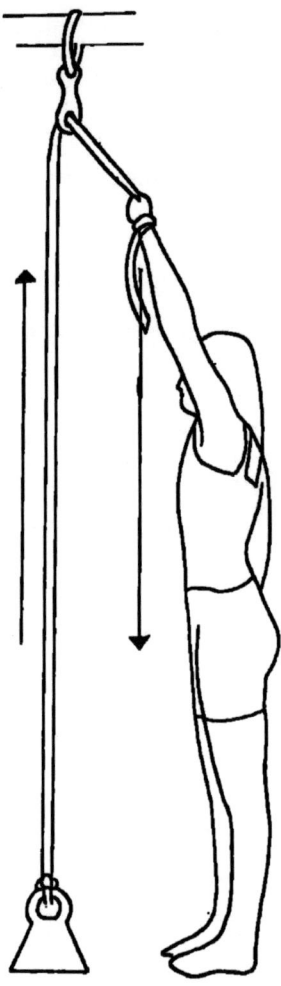

Figure 12. The poor man's swim bench

Once you have found your maximum comfortable weight, take a step to the side of the rope and using the same arm as before try to raise the same weight but this time with your hand must come down out to the side of your body. I guarantee that if you truly found your maximum weight as described above, this time you won't be able to lift it. So if you can't do it now, don't do it in the pool.

In the pool

The drag belt set up described in the arm recovery 'in the pool' section (page 69) obviously also works the pull action and all of the subsequent areas discussed in this Chapter. Watch out for your hand cutting through the water sideways instead of pulling against it. This is a sure sign that you have done enough. Your hand is effectively ducking out of the exertion of pulling and all you will do is to ruin your stroke technique if you continue.

The stomach for tumble turns

On page 35 I explained that a tumble turn is just an upside down sit-up. So there is definitely a need for sit-ups in the land power session. Because a tumble turn involves a twisting action I specifically recommend chinnies. These are sit-ups in which you twist and bring your right elbow to touch the outside of your left knee (raising your left knee up to meet it as you do so — Figure 13). You then, similarly, bring your left elbow to your right knee in the next sit-up and continue alternating thereafter. Try to twist as you rise, not to rise and then twist. Sets of 30 of these will work each side 15 times and you can increase the resistance by holding small weights in your hands.

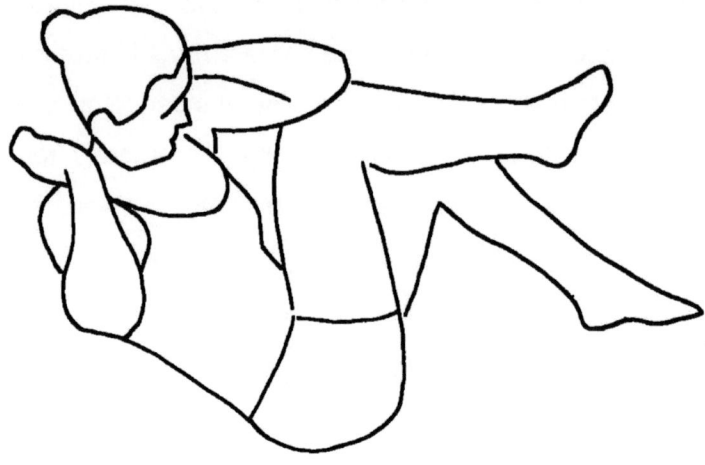

Figure 13. Chinnies

The hip drive

The action of driving your hip downwards under the water in order to throw your arm forwards above the water is difficult to isolate on land. There is an exercise which comes close but I have only ever seen it in one gym. It is a flat disc, about 40 cm in diameter, which you stand on with your feet fairly close together and swing to the left and right alternately by twisting at the hips. Presumably one could increase the resistance by holding some weights at the same time, but having never tried it I am not qualified to recommend it. The only solution available is to do resistance training in the pool (with a drag belt as described) and single out the hip drive action in your mind.

The legs for starts and turns

The only really crucial power exercise remaining is either Squat jumps which have been described earlier in this Chapter (Figure 10) or Cleans (These are the first part of the 'Clean and Jerk' and require qualified instruction – see www.momentumsports.co.uk).

Training for power

These will help speed up both starts and turns. Again, lower calf flexibility (page 80) helps you to exercise the quads (front thighs) throughout their length and make the most of what is a very powerful muscle group.

10

Flexibility

Part I of this book demonstrates that flexibility, in certain specific areas of the body, is fundamental to successful sprinting. Improved flexibility, or maintenance of current flexibility, is achieved through stretching and massage. Stretching is also necessary for injury prevention.

While flexibility in some muscle sets is critical to swimming, in other areas it is of very little relevance. Some parts of the body respond fairly quickly to stretching and massage but others take a lot of time and perseverance, so make sure that you are convinced of the relevance before dedicating time to it. As explained below, it is far better to spend an hour concentrating on a few specific areas than an hour trying to do every stretch under the sun for only a few seconds each.

Before I list those stretches I consider to be relevant, there are a few basic rules that will help you reap the benefits much quicker.

The muscles have got to be warmed up before you start
When I was at school we would touch our toes and bounce slightly as we did it, e.g. ten times. There was no warm-up beforehand; it generally was the warm up for something else. By the time I was at University bouncing, or ballistic stretching as it is properly called, had fallen out of favour because the jerky action simply makes the muscles contract and a tense muscle cannot be stretched effectively. The new advice was to hold the stretch statically (i.e.

still) *but to warm up beforehand.* It is now widely accepted that the range of movement of joints is enhanced by high core body temperatures. (Incidentally, a raised body temperature also allows a muscle to contract more forcefully, relax more quickly and receive more oxygen. All of which has got to be useful for sprinting!) With this advice in mind most athletes started to do static stretching sessions, to improve/maintain their flexibility, *after* their training sessions, safe in the knowledge that they were well warmed up. This is still the best advice hence my inclusion of post-training flexibility sessions on page 59. However, with regards to the pre-training, injury prevention stretches, nowadays the advice from those in the know is that stretching should be dynamic. Dynamic simply means involving movement. A movement that closely replicates the action about to be undertaken (i.e. sport specific) is considered to be better than a static stretch.

The structure of a training session should therefore be as follows:
- Warm-up swim of at least 200 m
- A short set of dynamic stretching in the shallow end
- A preliminary technique set
- Main set
- Warm down
- Post-training static stretches in tracksuits

I must confess that some of my warm up stretches are still static because I have yet to think of ways to make them dynamic though I am trying as you will see.

Hold static stretches for a long time at your comfortable maximum stretch

The trouble is that inherently competitive people tend to compete with themselves as well as others. They will try to hold a stretch at the maximum possible extension that they can, despite the pain, which they are used to enduring in training anyway. The problem with this is that the pain leads to tension and you cannot stretch a muscle effectively if it is under tension. It needs to be relaxed. Time and patience are the virtues required here. A static stretch should be held just on the edge of comfort for a minimum of 20 seconds but more ideally for one minute plus in a position you could almost doze off in (in true yoga fashion). If the pain doesn't ease off, you're pushing it too hard.

Do it regularly

If you're going to make serious inroads you've got to stretch at least five days out of seven, which means that you are far more likely to succeed if you pick a few exercises and set aside an amount of time that is achievable on a daily basis.

Areas to concentrate

Again, Part I can be used to identify the key **areas** to concentrate. This time they are in no particular order because natural flexibility varies so much from person to person.

Flexibility

The 'pecs' (The pectorals link your upper arms to the front of your chest)

Why   To enable you to remove your hand completely form the water without raising the centre of your chest and moving your head (Figure 2, page 14).

How (static)   Straighten each arm out behind you. It helps to have something to hold on to e.g. a door frame (Figure 14).

(dynamic)   Do forwards arm circles concentrating on stretching the pecs each time you come around to the backwards position. (You can also do it with your elbow bent to stop your hand hitting the water if you are standing in the pool).

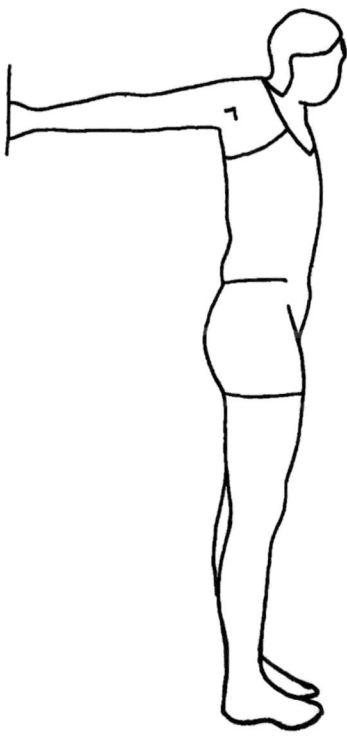

Figure 14. Stretching the pecs statically

The hamstrings (backs of your upper legs)

Why — Stability and response time for starts (page 32)

How (static) — Sit down on the floor with your legs out straight in front of you. Lean forwards and latch your fingers around your feet. Aim eventually to get your head on to your knees. This way is the most relaxed because you are sitting down and I find flexibility improves quicker if you have something to latch on to to maintain the stretch.

(dynamic) — Stand on one leg and swing the other one backwards and forwards keeping it straight.

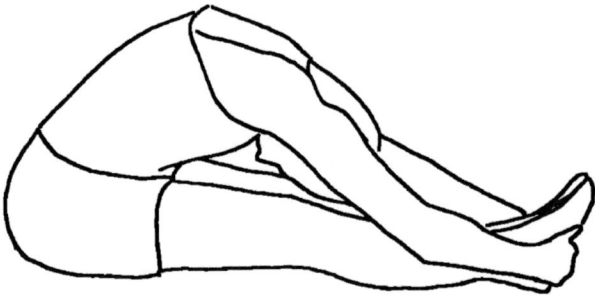

Figure 15. Stretching the hamstrings statically

The soleus (deep calves)

Why — An advantageous position on the starting blocks (page 33), possibly more powerful turns (page 39) and prevents calf cramps during training.

How (static) — Stand facing a wall with the toes of one foot approximately 5 to 10 cm away from it. Bend the corresponding knee until it touches the wall. Once the knee is on the wall, the wall bears some of your weight helping you to relax. (Figure 16).

Flexibility

(dynamic)   Standing up with your legs fairly close together, step each foot backwards in turn, bending your leg fully at the knee as you do so.

Figure 16. Stretching the soleus statically

(massage)   Calves need a lot of work to improve their flexibility, so a bit of self-massage helps a lot and there's an easy way to do it. You need a large cylindrical roller which you can buy purpose built for the job, but a rolling pin works just as well.

Sit on the floor with your legs stretched out in front of you. Place the roller under your lower calf and push your whole leg backwards and forwards on top of it. Note that during massage pressure is always applied towards the heart only to avoid damaging the valves in the venous blood vessels, so push hard only as the roller moves up your leg. You can apply greater pressure by placing one leg on top of the other*.

The deltoids (back of the arms at the top)

Why — These muscles are heavily used in pulling your arm out of the water and holding it high while you throw it forwards (page 68). Unless stretched regularly they can get very tight and painful and you will gradually lose the use of the full length of muscle. Sometimes, on TV, you see competitors in their pre-race rituals relaxing and then gently shaking their deltoids. They always look incredibly lose and supple. I am never quite sure whether they are showing off to 'psych out' the opposition, or genuinely loosening them off!

How (static) — Keeping it straight, raise your left arm across your chest so that your hand is pointing to your right. Link your right arm in front of it and pull towards you (Figure 17). To get even more stretch stand facing a wall and lean forwards against it.

(dynamic) — Keeping it straight, raise your left arm across your chest but don't link your right arm in front of it, keep it out wide. Then swap so that your right arm is across your chest and your left arm is out wide. Keep swinging your arms backwards and forwards keeping your back as still as possible.

---

* For more information on massage see *Sport and Remedial Massage Therapy*. 1996. Mel Cash. Ebury Press.

Flexibility

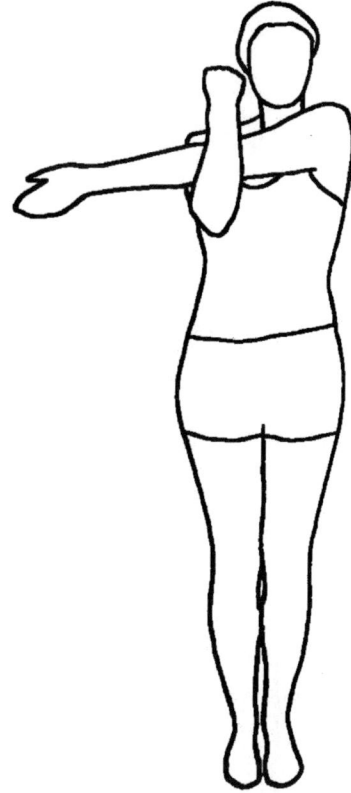

Figure 17. Stretching the backs of the arms statically

The quads (front upper thigh)

Why   For starts and turns.

How (static)   You can stand up and hold your heel against your bum to stretch these, but you are likely to stretch for longer if you are relaxed and lying on the floor (Figure 18). Tuck the leg to be stretched up under your bum. You can stretch both legs at the same time but if you feel pressure on your back tuck your arms behind you to support it. Afterwards, stay lying on your back but hugging your knees and that will relax it.

Speed Demon

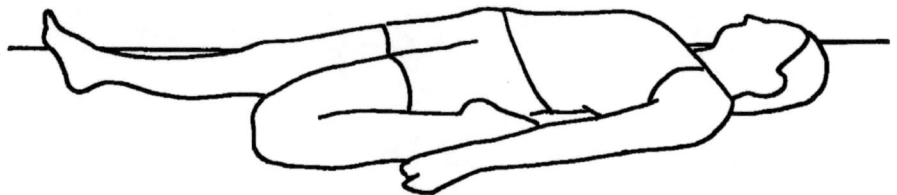

Figure 18. Stretching the quads statically

Upper back, behind the shoulder blades and the back of the neck

Why   Remember how rest was the first skill in the tool kit. One of the most common causes of an inability to sleep is tension in the back of the neck and shoulders. If you don't sleep well you won't recover properly.

How (static)   This is a yoga position called 'the plough'. After a bit of practice this is so comfortable you can almost fall asleep in it.

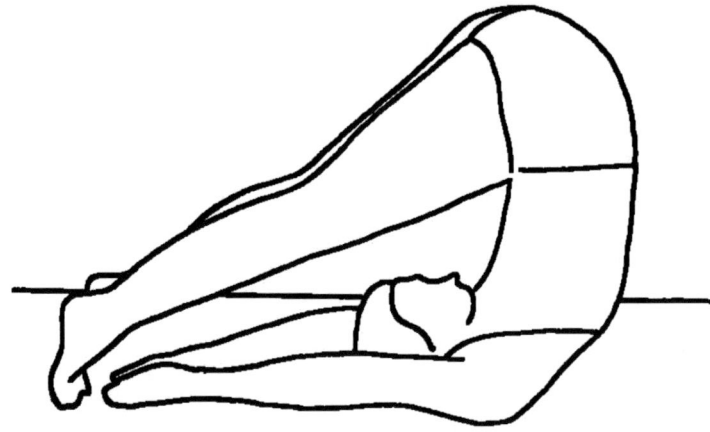

Figure 20. The plough

Lie on your back with your arms stretched out above your head. (You may need some padding behind your neck). Lift your legs up and over your head. The first position to aim for is balancing your knees on your forehead. Once you're comfortable there you can move on to either getting your knees by your arm pits, or your legs stretched out behind you (Figure 20).

Closing statement

I once overheard a national standard distance swimmer turn to her friend and say '50's are easy. You don't have to pace yourself. You put your head down and go for it'. I hope that in reading this book you have seen how wrong she was. Sprint freestyle races may be short but there's plenty of thinking to do. Don't imagine for one minute that top class swimmers were just born that way and are lucky enough to do it all naturally. Some lucky people do exist, but their times are highly erratic because they can't pin down in their conscious minds what it is that they are doing. To produce consistently high quality races you have to know. You cannot leave it to chance. I know an athlete who was once one of the fastest 400 m hurdlers in the country. After every race he knew which leg had been his lead leg on each of the ten hurdles and exactly how many strides he had taken between them all. He had this information in the forefront of his mind during a race and was constantly analysing it and responding to it throughout, even though it only lasted around 50 seconds. My races in those days were just blurs. I did just dive in and do it. At the end I wouldn't even know which arm I'd turned on. If you want to succeed it cannot be like that. The greatest skill you must acquire, beyond all those listed in this book, is an ability to apply your mind to the task at hand. Think. Question everything. Solve problems and then think some more.

Appendix A

Building a sprint stroke — The stroke technique set

Start with **6 x 25 m** at a comfortably fast arm speed. No legs yet. You want to feel the full effect of each additional focus point. As you move through the six swims get all the previous points correct first and then add in the one you are on. If you feel you didn't do one well, just have another go. It's not particularly rigid.

1. Keep your **head still**. Think of *nothing* else. If you breathe then return your head quickly.
2. Add in — make your **hand pull path central** (page 11) and **shallow** (page 25).
3. Add in — remembering that you are not doing these leisurely, **lengthen your stroke** by dropping your hips as far as you are willing to submerge your shoulder (page 22).
4. Add in— keep your **elbow high in the water** as you make your shallow, central pull (page 25).
5. Add in — think about your **hand entry**. Make it the **correct width** (page 16) and the **correct distance** in front of you (page 26).
6. Add in— **plunge your hand deep** before catching hold of the water (page 25) and when you have done so, **lock your wrist** (page 19).

Between each take three or four seconds rest, just enough to remind yourself of the next focus point and then go again.

Now that you've got the stroke right its time to add in some power. So do **2 x 25 m** (Still no legs and the same sort of rest or a couple of seconds more):

1. Make sure you finish the stroke powerfully by **driving your elbow out** of the water without moving your head (pages 13 and 68)
2. Focus on **driving each hip down** and feel it throw you arm forwards.

Finally build up to your full sprint by doing **3 more 25 m swims:**

1. Start slowly and **build up gradually to a flat-out arms-only sprint** by the time you finish. Get the stroke right in the first 10 m and then add the top speed in in the rest of the length.
2. Go straight into a **flat-out arms-only sprint but half way down the length gradually add in your sprint kick** and see if you can feel the point where your hands lose grip on the water.
3. Push off underwater, full throttle with your legs into a **flat-out full stroke** sprint. **Halfway down the length, switch off your legs for 5 to 6 strokes** and see if you feel your arms strengthen. Try to keep you arms 'in charge' by working them really hard but bring your legs back in gradually to finish the length.

Once you are familiar with all these checks you can represent each by a single word or phrase and develop mantras of the most effective ones in order of diminishing importance to you. Then, as you set off in a sprint you can chant them and check each in your mind. E.g: Head still, elbow drive, hip force etc. Eventually you'll find you do them without chanting. They are now in your subconscious and hey presto — you have *genuinely* improved your stroke.

Appendix B

Building a powerful turn – The turn technique set

This works in a similar way to the stroke set in that you build up a good turn by concentrating on each of its component parts in turn. I usually did a continuous swim with gentle breaststroke down the middle 15 m of the length and 90% speed freestyle sprints into and out of each turn, concentrating on each focus point in the order they were made in Part I. They were:

1. The almighty **final arm pull.**
2. Putting your **chin on your chest.**
3. **Throwing your legs over** from the hips.
4. Making the **foot-plant position** two o'clock or ten o'clock (to avoid a banana turn).
5. Getting your **heels on the wall** if it works for you.
6. Keeping your **head tucked** through out your push off.
7. **Surfacing quickly**.
8. Making the **first stroke on the side of the dipped hip.**

Acknowledgements

Many thanks to Pete Baldrey for giving up his time to go through the text with me. In fact, thanks to all those in the swimming fraternity who have helped me along the way and are too numerous to mention. But most of all thanks to Richard who opened the door.

Lightning Source UK Ltd.
Milton Keynes UK
02 November 2009

145712UK00001B/277/P